TRANSFORM YOUR
K-5 MATH CLASS

Digital Age Tools to Spark Learning

AMANDA THOMAS

International Society for Technology in Education
PORTLAND, OREGON • ARLINGTON, VIRGINIA

Transform Your K–5 Math Class
Digital Age Tools to Spark Learning
Amanda Thomas

Editor: *Emily Reed*
Copy Editor: *Camille Cole*
Proofreader: *Lynda Gansel*
Indexer: *Valerie Haynes Perry*
Book Design and Production: *Kim McGovern*
Cover Design: *Edwin Ouellette*

Library of Congress Cataloging-in-Publication Data available

First Edition
ISBN: 978-1-56484-802-4
Ebook version available.

Printed in the United States of America

About ISTE

The International Society for Technology in Education (ISTE) is a nonprofit organization that works with the global education community to accelerate the use of technology to solve tough problems and inspire innovation. Our worldwide network believes in the potential technology holds to transform teaching and learning.

ISTE sets a bold vision for education transformation through the ISTE Standards, a framework for students, educators, administrators, coaches and computer science educators to rethink education and create innovative learning environments. ISTE hosts the annual ISTE Conference & Expo, one of the world's most influential edtech events. The organization's professional learning offerings include online courses, professional networks, year-round academies, peer-reviewed journals and other publications. ISTE is also the leading publisher of books focused on technology in education. For more information or to become an ISTE member, visit iste.org. Subscribe to ISTE's YouTube channel and connect with ISTE on Twitter, Facebook and LinkedIn.

Also by the Author

Transform Your 6–12 Math Class: Digital Tools to Spark Learning

Related ISTE Titles

Coding + Math: Strengthen K–5 Math Skills with Computer Science

About the Author

Amanda Thomas, Ph.D., is an assistant professor of mathematics education in the Department of Teaching, Learning and Teacher Education at University of Nebraska–Lincoln. She received her doctoral degree in 2013 from the University of Missouri–Columbia. Her research focuses on teachers' use of mobile technology in elementary math classrooms. She's also interested in STEM education and supporting teachers in innovative STEM integration.

Acknowledgments

This book was shaped by countless influences, interactions, and individuals who contributed to my vision for math teachers' strategic use of technology in the classroom. Although the cases in the book are fictitious approximations of practice, they were inspired by the practices and challenges shared by countless classroom teachers, preservice teachers, and students over the course of many years. I am grateful for their collective inspiration and insight.

I am also appreciative of my friend and colleague, A.J. Edson, without whom this book would not exist. Our long-term collaboration around technology and mathematics education—and A.J.'s early involvement in the proposal and visioning stages—helped bring this project to fruition. My colleagues and students at the University of Nebraska, Lincoln provide ongoing support for my work. In particular, I thank Lorraine Males for her friendship and guidance, Guy Trainin and Al Steckelberg for their mentorship, Kara Viesca for her insights about book authorship, and Kelley Buchheister for her feedback throughout the writing process and her all-around camaraderie.

This book draws upon the prior work of researchers in technology and math education and I am thankful for the opportunity to build on their work with the support of ISTE and the editors with whom I have worked. I am grateful to Valerie Witte who initiated this project and provided guidance throughout the process, and Emily Reed whose support and feedback led to a finished product that I hope will be useful for technology and math educators.

Dedication

For my family. I dedicate this book to my husband, Michael and adult children, Lexi and Quinton, who have been on this journey with me for decades, and to Leighton and Renden who I hope will enjoy the kinds of math learning experiences envisioned in this book.

Contents

Contents

INTRODUCTION

DIGITAL TOOLS OPEN NEW HORIZONS for learning math. Can math be taught effectively without technology? Sure, it has been for centuries. Can we reasonably expect digital tools to transform a classroom where math is narrowly defined and taught in ways that are inequitable or ineffective? Research and practice tell us no. The question, then, is how can digital tools be integrated in a way that adds value to math classes? When combined with effective teaching practices and interesting, rigorous math content, technology can be a transformative force in the classroom.

This book promotes a vision and path toward transformative use of digital tools to spark learning in elementary (K–5) math classrooms. This book begins with a series of instead of ..., what if... contrasts to spark imagination about what technology could do in math classrooms. Chapter one explores relevant context, standards, considerations, and challenges. Chapters two through six feature cases and vignettes of technology use in elementary math classrooms. These chapters also provide prompts for reflection and discussion, and connections with research. Chapter seven summarizes the big ideas presented throughout the various classroom cases.

During the course of this book, technology is defined broadly. Some cases highlight math-specific technologies. Others focus on generalized digital tools being used strategically to support math teaching and learning. This book is not a "how to" manual for any particular technologies. Many valuable publications of that nature already exist. Instead, it is an opportunity to think about how a variety of digital tools could be used effectively to teach math in the K–5 classroom. The cases and vignettes feature a spectrum of technology availability, from a single-teacher device used to facilitate math discussions, to shared devices and 1:1 student technologies. As you read this book, think about the technology tools that are highlighted, the math and teaching practices they support, and how you might implement or adapt these for your own context.

Connecting Classroom Practice with Research

The goal of this book is to bridge research and practice regarding educational technology and math teaching and learning, as illustrated in Figure 0.1.

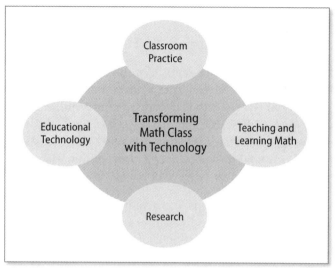

Figure 0.1 Bridging research and practice in math and technology.

By combining what we've learned from research on the subject of best practices in the applications of educational technology in teaching math in K–5 grade levels, we can begin to develop transformative, technology-rich teaching and learning experiences. We can consider technology and math standards that are based on research and impact practice.

Instead of …, What if …?

Oxford Dictionaries defines *transformative* as "causing a marked change in someone or something." When implementing digital tools to transform elementary math classrooms, we consider the status quo and possibilities for marked changes. Perceived barriers to transformation are also considered, including required curriculum, access to technology, and time needed to learn how to use the technology tools. Of course, there are wide variations in the status quo among classrooms, so this book considers a series of *instead of …, what if …* scenarios that contrast frequently seen uses of technology with bolder possibilities. In these scenarios, we combine a variety of digital tools with best practices for teaching math. These contrasting scenarios include:

- Instead of technology used as a gimmick for "tricking" students into learning math, what if technology was used as an instructional tool to enhance learning of rich math content?

- Instead of using screens for disconnected, individualized learning, what if technology enabled mathematical discourse and collaboration?

- Instead of using technology to assess what students *don't* know about math, what if we used technology to understand and build upon what students *do* know?

- Instead of teacher-centered instruction that includes technology, what if we leveraged the interactivity powers of technology to empower student-driven learning?

- Instead of technology for its own sake, what if we used technology in the service of teaching and learning rich, interesting math?

Chapters two through six each begin with contrasting cases that suggest how technology could be transformative in a K–5 math class. One case that describes what often is, and another that illustrates what could be.[1] The comparisons are not meant to be critical or evaluative of established practice, but rather the intent is to present alternatives for educators who want to combine innovative technology use with effective math teaching practices. Nevertheless, transformative cases are still imperfect. You may think of more innovative or transformative uses of technology for similar topics; or, the ideas presented in these cases may be replaced by new possibilities enabled by future tools and technologies. These are meant to prompt thought and discussion about how technology can combine with effective math teaching—the primary purpose of these contrasting cases.

You will find reflection and discussion prompts for each of the cases. If you're reading this book on your own, take a moment to think about how the cases presented relate to your own practice and to the big ideas in this book. If you're reading as part of a book club or professional development experience involving other teachers, consider using the prompts to discuss and unpack the important aspects of each case.

Once you've had a chance to read and reflect on the contrasting cases, you'll find that each chapter highlights what current research has to say about those topics. Each chapter concludes with a summary and recommendations for classroom practice as well as alignment with math content and practice standards, and ISTE

Standards for students and educators. You may find it meaningful to consider how the cases align with standards in your state. If you are reading this book as part of a professional development program, it may be a useful exercise to begin by aligning the cases with relevant standards, and then comparing your alignment with what the author has proposed at the end of each chapter. Whether you are reading this book individually, for your own interest, or with others as part of a professional development experience, take the opportunity to compare each case with your own technology use and math teaching practices. Consider what is and what could be in your own classroom!

1   All individuals and situations in case vignettes are fictional and represent a synthesis of the author's observations and experience in math classroom settings.

CONSIDERATIONS AND CHALLENGES FOR INTEGRATING TECHNOLOGY IN MATH TEACHING

How technology is integrated into one's teaching practices is connected to the models of teaching and approaches to learning that are employed.

THIS CHAPTER INCLUDES overviews of relevant considerations and challenges for integrating digital tools into math instruction in Grades K–5. These considerations and challenges include a working definition for school math as a socially-constructed endeavor, including equity and access to cutting-edge technology, 1:1 technology initiatives, curriculum resources, and personalized learning. The chapter concludes with a discussion of standards that frame technology and math in elementary classrooms.

What Is School Math?

To many, math is a set of numbers, symbols, formulas, and rules. Others might think of school math in terms of subtopics such as arithmetic, geometry, algebra, and statistics. Mathematicians tend to focus on such things as patterns, structure, logic, proof, modeling, and abstractions. Math content standards have defined specific math learning expectations, as well as standards for math practice that articulate mathematical ways of thinking.

This book draws upon the National Research Council's conception of mathematical proficiency as described in the 2001 book, *Adding it Up: Helping Children Learn Mathematics*. This vision of learning math consists of five interwoven, interdependent threads: conceptual understanding, procedural fluency, strategic competence, adaptive reasoning, and productive disposition. Success in school math has often overemphasized procedural fluency; hence the interpretation of math as numbers, symbols, formulas, and rules. Although being fluent with procedures and algorithms is important, so too are understanding the underlying concepts and connections, formulating problems and choosing useful strategies to solve them, justifying and adapting logical reasoning, and approaching math as a subject worth learning. Technology can and should support all strands of math proficiency, but a quick glance at the market for math apps reveals an abundance of drill and practice applications that emphasize procedural fluency. There are far fewer apps that help develop other strands of proficiency. Although a drill and practice app might be easy to pick up and play, many of the apps that support deeper reasoning and conceptual understanding are most valuable in combination with interesting math problems. Considering all strands of math proficiency can help you, the teacher, make more effective technology choices for your students' learning needs.

Math Learning Is a Socially Constructed Endeavor

When we interpret math proficiency as a combination of procedures, concepts, strategies, reasoning, and disposition, developing math proficiency becomes more complex than numerical problems with multiple-choice answers. Traditional models of teaching math have included teacher-centered classrooms where students sat in rows of desks, listened and watched dutifully as the teacher demonstrated how to carry out a procedure, practiced the procedure with the teacher as a class, and then completed independent practice exercises that mimicked what the teacher modeled. This paradigm of instruction is sometimes referred to as *gradual release,* or *I do, We do, You do,* and tends to align with behavioristic transmission of knowledge from teacher to student.

More contemporary models of math teaching center students in their own learning and emphasize procedural fluency in connection with other strands of math proficiency. Rather than asking students to reproduce a demonstration done on the board, teachers monitor and support students as they grapple with challenging math tasks. Facilitating classroom discussions that elicit students' ideas and reasoning builds shared knowledge of concepts, strategies, and procedures. Partner and group work allow students to communicate mathematically and strengthen individual understanding through peer interactions. This model of teaching often employs a *reverse gradual release,* or *You do, We do, I do,* and facilitates classroom interactions that are more consistent with constructivist or sociocultural theories of learning that emphasize active learning in social contexts. How technology is integrated into one's teaching practices is connected to the models of teaching and approaches to learning that are employed.

Equity and Access to Technology and Math

It is not enough for some, or even most students to learn meaningful math and to have access to educational technology. Patterns of inequities disproportionately impact girls, children with special needs, and students from racially, ethnically, and linguistically diverse backgrounds, depriving them of rich learning opportunities. For example, diverse students tend to be overrepresented in "low" math tracks where they are too often met with low expectations and procedurally focused math that is not built on a foundation of conceptual understanding. Here, too, there are often fewer resources and less-experienced teachers.

Likewise, students often do not have equitable access to technology resources and technology-rich learning activities. Achievement gaps on national and international assessments, patterns of enrollment in remedial college math courses, and interest in STEM majors and careers, provide further evidence of these inequities. When considering how to integrate technology into math teaching and learning, it's not enough for *some* students to have access to tools and practices that can transform learning. Instruction should be designed so that each and every student has an opportunity to engage, participate, and develop a positive identity as a math learner.

1:1 Technology Initiatives

Student access to technology devices can be a major barrier for technology integration in math, or any subject. Many schools have been gradually transitioning from dedicated rooms for computer labs to mobile computer/tablet carts, and other options. Recently, we're seeing more 1:1 devices for each student. In some cases, students are issued their own laptop or tablet for an entire school year, or across multiple years. Other options include 1:1 computers that are kept in classrooms for use when teachers and students choose to use them, which is seemingly more common in elementary classrooms. Bring-your-own device (BYOD) initiatives encourage each student to bring their personal computer, tablet, or smartphone. BYOD devices that differ from student to student introduce new challenges for you, the teacher, who must plan across platforms. Overall, ubiquitous access to devices could expand the possibilities for what you and your students could accomplish.

Curriculum Resources

The widespread availability of online open educational resources (OERs) offers a number of advantages for schools, teachers, and students. Especially for schools already investing in 1:1 technologies, free OERs offer significant cost savings over printed textbooks and curriculum materials. Many OERs are customizable for teachers, so you can sequence, add, or omit online content to meet your instructional goals. For students, an obvious benefit of online curriculum resources is convenience. Instead of remembering and transporting multiple books, one digital device can house a wealth of resources. In addition to online resources, digital platforms enable teachers, or groups of teachers, to create their own curriculum resources. Digital instructional materials and OERs could democratize access to the creation, customization, and consumption of curriculum. But it's important to note that you, the teacher, must also become a careful curator and cautious consumer of online curriculum resources. In math, for example, comprehensive, coherent, standards-aligned, research-based curriculum materials require many years and a wealth of expertise to develop. Furthermore, free resources often do not go through the same vetting processes as traditionally-published materials.

Personalized Learning

The ISTE Standards for Educators specify that to personalize learning experiences, one should "Capitalize on technology's efficiencies and functionality to meet students' individual learning needs." Few would argue the value of this goal, which sounds a lot like using technology to differentiate instruction. A related idea, sometimes used synonymously with "personalized learning," is "individualized learning." Individual learning programs allow learners to progress through lessons and complete assessments at their own pace. For more than half a century, individualized learning has been tried in classrooms with and without digital technologies. Some of these early individualized learning efforts were called programmed instruction, a term coined by the well-known behaviorist, B.F. Skinner. Modern, technology-based individualized instruction programs may include adaptive assessment, multimedia content, and voluminous data points. One must question whether or not they are substantively different from programmed instruction. When personalized learning manifests as programmed instruction, teachers must grapple with managing dozens of students, each working on different material at different times, and subject matter becomes reduced to a series of skills-based inputs and outputs. This is hardly the conceptually rich, inquiry-based, authentic learning that you wish to promote. On the other hand, you can and should use technology to create, adapt, and personalize learning experiences in ways that meet students' diverse needs and identities.

Cutting-Edge Technologies

Coding tools, robots, drones, AI, 3D printers: new technologies present new opportunities! Embracing cutting-edge tools can be exciting and valuable for both you and your students. As some early adopters and innovative educators jump at the chance to incorporate the latest technologies, many have wrestled with how new tools could fit in with existing practices, curriculum, and standards. In addition to practical constraints of time, planning, and access to cutting-edge devices, other factors that impact teaching with new technologies include beliefs, knowledge, and attitudes about technology. Additional variables include subject matter and teaching methodologies. To realize the potential of innovative technologies for teaching and learning math, support is required when first learning how to incorporate new tools in combination with effective teaching practices.

Standards for Technology and Math

Technology integration and math teaching are guided and influenced by a variety of standards. The ISTE Standards for Students, Educators, Education Leaders, and Coaches (iste.org/standards) provide a framework for digital age learning across

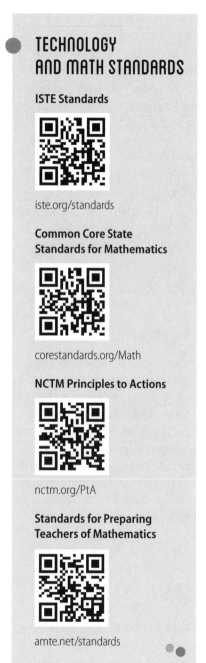

TECHNOLOGY AND MATH STANDARDS

ISTE Standards

iste.org/standards

Common Core State Standards for Mathematics

corestandards.org/Math

NCTM Principles to Actions

nctm.org/PtA

Standards for Preparing Teachers of Mathematics

amte.net/standards

all disciplines. In math, the Common Core State Standards for Mathematics have been adopted in 47 U.S. states and territories since 2010. In 2014, the National Council of Teachers of Mathematics (NCTM) released Principles to Actions: Ensuring Mathematical Success for All. These cross-cutting principles and effective teaching practices are helpful for implementing rigorous math standards. The Standards for Preparing Teachers of Mathematics, released in 2017 by the Association of Mathematics Teacher Educators (AMTE), describe a vision for math teachers. State- and district-level standards for technology and math add another layer of guidelines and expectations for math teachers.

Technology and math standards have been influential in education for nearly three decades. The 1989 Curriculum and Evaluation Standards for School Mathematics, 2000 Principles and Standards for School Mathematics, and 2006 Curriculum Focal Points—all from NCTM—help to provide a coherent, research-informed framework for math teaching and learning that is reflected in many state standards, math textbooks, teacher preparation, and professional development programs. Likewise, the National Education Technology Standards, introduced in 1998, helped to define the technology skills students need to develop. Subsequent standards for teachers (2000) and administrators (2001) articulated ways that stakeholders could support students' development of technology standards. In addition to providing professional recommendations and shaping educational policies, technology and math standards impact curriculum, teacher preparation, and professional development.

Although the standards for technology and math are largely separate documents, they do provide some guidance for integrating math and technology. Many of the ISTE standards cut across content areas, and their recent emphasis on computational thinking relates closely to expectations for teaching and learning math. The Common Core Standards for Mathematical Practice include an expectation that students *use appropriate tools strategically,* and specifically identifies how technologies can support school math instruction. NCTM includes technology among their cross-cutting principles, and AMTE standards include the competency C.1.6., *Use Mathematical Tools and Technology.* The intersection of priorities for teaching and learning math and technology are found in the standards and in recent STEM initiatives (in which technology and math account for half of the STEM acronym). Goals for technology and math teaching and learning have been established by a variety of stakeholders, but you, the teachers, are the ones who bring these goals to life in the classroom.

Considerations and challenges relevant to educational technology and math education frame this book's vision of technology-rich math teaching and learning. Of course, broader considerations and challenges can also impact technology integration. Issues such as quality professional development for teachers, school climate, technology support, teachers' knowledge and beliefs about technology and math, budget constraints for technology, and time constraints are beyond the scope of this book, but nevertheless important for teachers and stakeholders.

MOVING FROM GIMMICKS TO TOOLS FOR TEACHING RICH MATH

● Instead of using technology as a gimmick to "trick" students into
● learning math, what if technology is used as an instructional tool
● to enhance the learning of rich math concepts?

IN THIS CHAPTER, you will find two contrasting cases that illustrate teaching Grade 2 subtraction with technology tools. As you read each of the cases, consider how and what math is being taught, how technology is being used, and how these two ideas connect. After reading and reflecting on the two contrasting cases, compare your insights and connections with what research has to say about the two big ideas illustrated in the cases: *Technology as a Motivational Tool* and *Teaching Practices that Support Mathematical Learning*. Also take a moment to examine how each of the lessons align with standards for math content, math practices; and ISTE Standards for students, educators, and coaches. Standards alignment is offered at the end of the chapter for your reference.

Technology as a Motivational Tool

It is accepted that many students love technology. We see evidence of this when they play computer games, negotiate for more screen time, or engage on social media. Although this may not hold true for all students, it is common to use technology as a motivator to capture their attention, reward good behavior, or provide a context for learning that they will enjoy. When integrating technology into the teaching of a math lesson, look for ways to get students excited about content they may struggle with or dislike. Although it is true that interesting contexts and approaches to learning math can include or be facilitated by technology, it can be used as more than a gimmick or an add-on. Effective integration of technology into a math lesson starts with rich math content and effective math teaching practices. Technology is a tool to enhance the teaching and learning of math, not a distraction or a trick that does not align with what research tells us about technology and its relationship with teaching and learning math.

Teaching Practices that Support Math Learning

Doing math is more than carrying out algorithms. Teaching practices that support math learning develop fluency by drawing on students' conceptual understanding, offering opportunities for making connections among multiple representations and strategies, and clarifying student thinking. Math teaching that rushes toward fluency without a foundation of conceptual understanding and number sense can be counterproductive. As we look for opportunities to integrate technology into math teaching, it is important that it supports what research tells us about how children learn math.

The following cases demonstrate different approaches to teaching with technology in the math classroom. Questions for discussion after each of the cases help examine what is working in the lesson and what could be done differently.

 CASE 2.1

Ms. Stenberg's Grade 2 Subtraction Lesson

OBJECTIVES
- Subtract two-digit numbers with regrouping using an algorithm.

Ms. Stenberg has six computers in the back of her second-grade classroom. Today she is teaching a lesson on subtraction of two-digit numbers where regrouping is necessary. From past years, she knows that many students struggle with this topic. She also knows that many of this year's students enjoy playing math games on one of the school-approved websites.

To start her lesson, she announces that students who demonstrate appropriate behavior throughout class, and finish their work on time, will earn computer time at the end of class. She then poses three warm-up subtraction problems:

$$45 - 31 = \underline{\hspace{1cm}} \qquad 96 - 55 = \underline{\hspace{1cm}} \qquad 82 - 64 = \underline{\hspace{1cm}}$$

As she anticipated, many students are struggling with the third problem. She gives them two more minutes to finish, and then asks them to check their answers with a table partner. She notices that Naomi has done the third problem correctly. After students exchange their answers, Ms. Stenberg invites Naomi to the board to show the class how she solved 82 – 64. Naomi rewrites the problem vertically and demonstrates how she solved the problem. See Figure 2.1.

Ms. Stenberg points to Naomi's work as she explains the steps used to subtract. She then uses the projector to display four more subtraction problems from a prepared slide on her computer. She shows students how to solve the four problems, explaining each step, asking questions such as, "What's next?" and "What do I get when I do that?" to invite students to participate. After each problem, she asks students if they have any questions, and addresses questions by re-explaining the step that seems to confuse students.

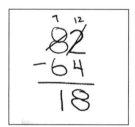

Figure 2.1 Naomi's subtraction work.

After demonstrating and explaining how to solve the subtraction problems, Ms. Stenberg passes out a worksheet containing subtraction problems. She asks all students to solve the first row of three problems, and to then raise their hands so she can check their work. The first six students who raise their hands with correct solutions are given the chance to play a subtraction game on the computers in the back of the classroom. Before class, she selected and bookmarked games for students. One of the games has students solve two-digit subtraction problems represented by regrouping within a basketball context. Students can earn two or three points for correct answers (depending on the difficulty), and each time the graphics show they have made a basket. If students answer incorrectly, they miss the basket and are given another try. Scrap paper and pencils are next to each computer to help students figure out the problems.

While the first six students play the subtraction game on the computers, she continues to check student work. When they've solved the first row of problems correctly, they are asked to continue with the rest of the worksheet. Every five minutes, she calls back the students from the computers to finish their worksheets and sends six new students to the computers. This gives her a chance to work one-on-one with students struggling with problems on the worksheet, and to keep a closer eye on those who are having trouble working productively until math time is over.

Reflection Questions

Consider Ms. Stenberg's use of technology in this lesson. Based on her perception of students' needs and preferences, she selected a computer game that aligned with the lesson content. She also used her computer and projector to display the problems on the board. Ask yourself the following questions as you reflect on the lesson:

- Would you consider this a technology-rich lesson? Why or why not?

- What was the purpose of Ms. Stenberg's technology use in this lesson?

- How did Ms. Stenberg's integration of technology advance the teaching and learning of math in this lesson?

- What were she and/or the students able to do with technology that was different from or better than what could have been done without technology?

Next, consider the math teaching practices in Ms. Stenberg's lesson.

- What were her goals for this math lesson?

- How did she address students' individual needs in this lesson?

- Would you describe this lesson as more teacher-centered or more student-centered? Why?

- To what extent did students have equitable access to learn and demonstrate their understanding of the lesson?

- Overall, what strengths do you see in this lesson? What opportunities do you notice?

● ● ● ●

Ms. Vaughan's second-grade class is also learning about two-digit subtraction with regrouping. As you read about Ms. Vaughan's lesson, consider how she integrates technology into the lesson and her math teaching practices.

✚ CASE 2.2

Ms. Vaughan's Grade 2 Subtraction Lesson

OBJECTIVES
* Use base ten blocks to accurately model subtraction with regrouping.
* Connect standard algorithm for subtraction with base ten models.

Ms. Vaughan launches the lesson by asking students to model 46 – 25 with base ten blocks, and then write the equation and solution. Students work individually at their seats to model this subtraction with a virtual base-block manipulative on their laptops, recording their equation and solution on paper. As students work, the teacher circulates around the room, monitoring students' work, addressing questions, and requesting that students with inaccurate models or equations compare and discuss their work with a neighboring student (specifically referring them to peers who she observed to have accurate models and equations).

Ms. Vaughan then poses the following problem aloud:

> Model 32 – 18 with base ten blocks. Then write the equation and solution on paper.

Students work in pairs using virtual manipulatives to solve the subtraction problem. While students are working, Ms. Vaughan observes their work and addresses questions and misconceptions. She expects to see some students struggle with taking away 8 ones, because there are only 2 ones initially represented. To these students, she asks questions such as, "Do you have more than eight ones? Do you have more than eight altogether? Is there anything you could do to get more ones? How do you know you're still subtracting from 32?" She makes note of students' work and strategies so she can call on specific students during whole-group discussion.

After all student pairs have solved the problem, Ms. Vaughan initiates a whole-group discussion by inviting Antonio to show and explain how he began the problem.

As students share their base ten block images via screencast and explain their reasoning, the teacher develops a written record of their work on the board. The written record scaffolds toward the subtraction algorithm. Table 2.1 summarizes student explanations and images alongside Ms. Vaughan's written record and questions/prompts.

TABLE 2.1 Student Explanations and Ms. Vaughan's Record and Prompts

Student Explanation	Student Base Ten Block Images	Ms. Vaughan's Written Record	Ms. Vaughan's Questions and Prompts
Antonio: I grabbed 3 ten sticks and two ones to make 32.	Base ten block representations of 32.	32	Do all friends agree that Antonio's picture shows 32? If you agree, touch your nose. [Class agrees.] Antonio, please call on someone else to explain what's next.
Brigit: I needed to take away 18, but I didn't have enough ones to take away eight.	Tens and ones in 32.	32 −18	Hmm, that's interesting, Brigit. What could we do so that we have enough ones to take away, Cole? Can you show us with the blocks what you did to solve this problem?
Cole: We could trade one of our ten sticks for ten ones. **Cole:** Two tens and twelve ones.	Exchanging a ten for ten ones.	2 12 ~~32~~ −18	So you traded one of your ten sticks for ten more ones? How many tens and how many ones did you have then, Cole? Two tens and twelve ones. Desiree, can you explain to the class how the equation on the board, so far, shows the trade that Cole just explained?
Desiree: Well, you had 32 take away 18, but you traded one of the tens for ten ones.	Two tens and twelve ones.	②12 ~~32~~ −18	Can you circle the part of the equation that shows this trade? Ok, Eman, can you add on to what Desiree just explained? What happened to the ten we traded?

Continued

Student Explanation	Student Base Ten Block Images	Ms. Vaughan's Written Record	Ms. Vaughan's Questions and Prompts
Eman: The ten became ten ones right here (points to the base ten blocks). **Eman:** Oh, I put the ten stick in the trash (points at trash icon), and got ten ones instead.	Eman's representation of two tens and 12 ones.	2 12 (circled) 32 (crossed) −18	Ok, can you circle those ones in the base ten blocks and in the equation? So, I notice that your picture doesn't show the ten stick crossed out like Cole's did. What happened to it? Nod your head up and down if you understand what Desiree and Eman just explained to us. I see a couple of friends don't look as sure. Faiza, what question do you have?
Faiza: What happened to the two ones we started with? Why did you cross out the two? **Faiza:** Yes, they're right here. But you crossed out the two in the 32. **Faiza:** Twelve … oh! That's where the little twelve comes from. Ok.	Exchanging a ten and two ones for 12 ones.	2 12 (circled) 32 (crossed) −18	Interesting question! Do you still see the two ones we started with in the base ten blocks? How many ones do we have, in all, after we traded one of the tens? Did everyone hear what Faiza just discovered? After we traded a ten, we had twelve ones in all. We crossed out the two in the equation and wrote a twelve above it to show that we have twelve ones. Giorgia: Please show us what we could do now to subtract 18 from 32.
Giorgia: Now that we have twelve ones, we just take eight of them away. Then we have four ones left.	Subtracting eight ones.	2 12 32 (crossed) −18 4	Ok, when we subtract eight ones from twelve ones, we have four ones left. Hiram, what about the tens?
Hiram: There's two tens and you take away one of them. **Hiram:** Fourteen. [Pointing at base ten blocks] There's one ten and four ones left.	Subtracting eight ones and one ten.	2 12 32 (crossed) −18 14	And what is left after you do this subtraction? Hiram, thanks for explaining how the base ten blocks show fourteen is the difference when we subtract 18 from 32. Isa, could you explain how the equation shows that 32−18=14?

Continued

Student Explanation	Student Base Ten Block Images	Ms. Vaughan's Written Record	Ms. Vaughan's Questions and Prompts
Isa: We had 32 to start with, but that wasn't enough ones to take eight from. Then we traded a ten for some ones and crossed out the 32 and wrote the little two and twelve at the top to show the trade. Then you take twelve minus eight is four, and two minus one is one, so you have fourteen left. **Isa:** No, it's two tens minus one ten.	 Crossing out a ten and eight ones.	2 12 ~~32~~ −18 14	When you say two minus one is one, are those really ones? Exactly, it's two tens minus one ten. We can see that in the base ten blocks, but the equation also shows us that the two and one are tens because they're in the tens column.

Following the whole-group discussion, Ms. Vaughan projects three more problems. Students work with their partner to model these problems with base ten blocks and record steps in solving the equation (subtraction algorithm).

$$52 - 35 = \underline{\hspace{1cm}} \qquad 44 - 27 = \underline{\hspace{1cm}} \qquad 61 - 32 = \underline{\hspace{1cm}}$$

While students are working, Ms. Vaughan circulates and, using a stop-motion app on her tablet, takes photos of students' manipulative work and steps in their written equations. Within the app, she quickly turns the photos into a short stop-motion video that shows blocks and corresponding steps of the subtraction algorithm.

To conclude the lesson, she calls students to the carpeted area. During the transition, she connects her tablet to the projector. When all students are at the carpet, Ms. Vaughan displays the stop-motion video, providing the opportunity for students to watch it at least two times.

After watching the video, Ms. Vaughan asks students to explain what the video shows. Student explanations serve as a summary of what they learned in the lesson, namely to use base ten blocks to model subtraction with regrouping and connecting base blocks to an equation. She plans to launch tomorrow's lesson with a similar stop-motion video and then challenge students to create their own videos. These should demonstrate the connections between base ten block representations of two-digit subtraction with regrouping and the subtraction algorithm.

Reflection Questions

Consider Ms. Vaughan's use of technology in this lesson. As you reflect and discuss, take into account what happened in Ms. Vaughan's lesson, and how it compares with Ms. Stenberg's class.

- Would you consider this a technology-rich lesson? Why or why not?

- What was the purpose of Ms. Vaughan's technology use in this lesson?

- How did Ms. Vaughan's integration of technology advance the teaching and learning of math in this lesson?

- What were she and/or the students able to do with technology that was different from or better than what they could have done without technology?

Next, consider the math teaching practices in Ms. Vaughan's lesson, and how they compare with the practices in the first scenario.

- What were Ms. Vaughan's goals for this math lesson?

- How did she address students' individual needs?

- Would you describe this lesson as more teacher-centered, or more student-centered? Why?

- To what extent did students have equitable access to learn and demonstrate their understanding in this lesson?

- Overall, what strengths do you see in this lesson? What opportunities do you notice?

● ● ● ●

What Does the Research Say?

Following are research findings regarding technology as a motivator for learning math:

- Technology may well serve as an external motivator for some students, but that does not necessarily mean students will learn more effectively with technology. Studies of technology as a student motivator have found mixed, or weak, associations between technology use for learning math and motivation for learning math.

- The positive effects of technology on motivation for learning math have often been intertwined with features of constructivist teaching practices such as exploratory and collaborative learning. This further supports our contention that technology use should be considered in conjunction with research-based math teaching practices.

- External motivators can make classroom experiences more "fun" for students, but more fun does not necessarily mean more effective. The use of tools and contexts to motivate math learning must be purposefully connected to math concepts in ways that engage students to learn more deeply. In some cases, the use of "fun" tools can be little more than a diversion from math concepts.

The following math teaching practice support student learning:

- "To use mathematics effectively, students must be able to do much more than carry out mathematical procedures" (Martin, 2009, p. 165). Research tells us that when procedures are connected with and built upon a strong foundation of concepts, students will be better equipped to accurately apply procedures in new contexts. In fact, Build Procedural Fluency from Conceptual Understanding is identified by the National Council of Teachers of Mathematics as one of eight effective math teaching practices (NCTM, 2014).

- Learning math extends far beyond getting the right answer; it involves a complex network of knowledge, skills, abilities, and beliefs. Math proficiency, as defined by the National Research Council, is composed of five interwoven and interdependent strands: conceptual understanding, procedural fluency, strategic competence, adaptive reasoning, and productive disposition. Any teaching approach that focuses exclusively on procedural fluency does not address the breadth of what it means to become mathematically proficient.

- Procedural and computational fluency is related to students' number sense and understanding of math structure. At the elementary level, facility with procedures for adding, subtracting, multiplying, and dividing whole numbers relates with students' understanding of place value concepts, composing and decomposing numbers, and properties of operations. This means it is important to give students opportunities to connect procedures with these concepts.

- Although a variety of gimmicks are often used to encourage and motivate students to learn math facts and develop procedural fluency, rushing toward fluency can have an opposite effect. Mathematical understanding takes time, and too early of an emphasis on fluency can result in math anxiety and a loss of interest in the subject. Thus, technology use that rushes fluency before students have a solid conceptual foundation may result in the opposite motivational effect many teachers intend.

Reflecting on Technology in Math Teaching

As you read the cases of Ms. Stenberg's and Ms. Vaughan's second-grade classrooms, you should have noticed significant differences in how the math was taught and how technology was used to support the teaching. In Ms. Stenberg's class, she aligned her technology use toward a behavioral goal of motivating students to complete the lesson, and a content goal of practicing subtraction algorithmically. Ms. Vaughan aligned her technology use with a goal to connect among multiple representations of subtraction (base ten block models, equations, and verbal explanations). Although she did not express a behavioral goal for the use of technology, we can note that it was used as a tool to facilitate participation and mathematical discourse throughout the lesson. In both cases, we see evidence of alignment between goals and use of technology for teaching and learning math. However, although well-intentioned, Ms. Stenberg's goals do not necessarily align with what research tells us about teaching and learning math, or about using technology for motivation in math. This helps to illustrate that aligning technology use with teaching, learning, and content goals is important, but may not be sufficient if those goals do not promote effective teaching and learning of rich math. Table 2.2 compares the use of technology in the two cases.

A helpful lens for considering Ms. Stenberg and Ms. Vaughan's technology use in these lessons might be to ask, *"How does the use of technology in this lesson advance students' opportunity to learn meaningful math?"* If the math lesson does not offer opportunities to learn meaningful math, then it is unrealistic to expect that technology could transform student learning experiences in ways that align with what we know from research.

TABLE 2.2 Use of Technology in the Cases of Ms. Stenberg and Ms. Vaughan

	The Case of Ms. Stenberg	The Case of Ms. Vaughan
What technology is used?	Math subtraction game on shared devices	Virtual base ten blocks, screencasting, stop-motion video on shared or 1:1 devices and teacher projected device
What math is emphasized?	Carrying out and practicing subtraction algorithm for two-digit numbers with regrouping	Connecting a visual model of subtraction with regrouping the steps of the subtraction algorithm
How is the lesson launched?	Ms. Stenberg announces a computer game as a behavioral motivator at the beginning of the lesson, and then asks students to solve subtraction problems and share their solutions with a peer.	Ms. Vaughan asks students to model a subtraction problem (without regrouping) using base ten blocks and to share with a peer as needed.
Who is doing the math in this lesson?	Ms. Stenberg demonstrates the procedure as students follow along and practice these procedures.	Students use familiar base-ten blocks to model subtraction with regrouping, and share their thinking with the rest of the class to build shared understanding.
When and how is technology used in the lesson?	Students can play a computer game at the end of their work.	Students use virtual manipulatives to model subtraction, and present their thinking to the class using projected screencasting software. The teacher displays a stop-motion video at the end of the lesson.

It is also important to consider the role technology plays in providing equitable access to learning math. In the case of Ms. Stenberg, students who met the objective first had first access to technology, while those who struggled the most were last to use the computers. (Furthermore, the computer game seemed to be part of a rush to computational fluency that does not align with what research tells us about learning math.) If we view technology as a reward for students who are already successful in math, we diminish the opportunity for technology to serve as a tool for supporting learning for those who may need it most. On the other hand, students in Ms. Vaughan's classroom each used technology early in the lesson to model subtraction and to connect between place value concepts and an algorithm. Each and every student had an opportunity to use technology as a tool for connecting among multiple representations; not as an add-on, but as a main part of the learning experience. The class discussion then engaged many students in sharing and explaining their representations and connections. Although students could have also used physical manipulatives for much of this activity, the use of virtual manipulatives facilitated the sharing of students' representations. (Once norms and expectations for devices are well-established, virtual manipulatives may require less materials management than physical versions). Unlike Ms. Stenberg, Ms. Vaughan's classroom benefited from 1:1 technology devices. In classrooms such as Ms. Stenberg's where the number of devices is limited, it is important to use sharing and grouping strategies that allow equitable access for all students rather than a select few.

Recommendations for Practice

At the beginning of this chapter, we posed the following question: *Instead of using technology as a gimmick to "trick" students into learning math, what if technology is used as an instructional tool to enhance the learning of rich math concepts?* The cases offer examples of what this shift might look like in an elementary classroom. But what can you do to effectively motivate rich math learning with technology in your classroom? Here are three suggestions with accompanying elaboration and examples.

1. Establish math learning goals that emphasize conceptual understanding and developing fluency from understanding.

Then, select technologies that align with those goals and are accessible to students. Implement apps and games that emphasize skill and drill only after students have developed understanding. Drill should increase speed and automaticity, but does little to support students who don't understand the math in the first place.

For example, when students are learning to divide whole numbers by fractions, a learning goal might be to efficiently and accurately divide whole numbers by fractions using the invert and multiply algorithm. A quick online search of "divide whole number by fraction game" yields thousands of possible games that quiz students' algorithmic fluency in potentially fun contexts, but without any representational or conceptual connections. Although it's easy to find many games that align with the previously stated goal, neither the games nor the goal provide students with an opportunity to develop conceptual understanding of fraction division.

Although it is important that students are eventually able to compute efficiently and accurately, they should first experience multiple opportunities to develop an understanding of fraction division. Consider an earlier goal such as "Represent division of whole numbers by unit fractions (a , 1/b) by modeling how many groups of size 1/b are contained in a." In this case, one might seek games that feature visual models (e.g., SplashMath's Divide Whole by a Unit Fraction or IXL's L.1 Divide whole numbers by unit fractions using models). Technology aligned with this goal might also include virtual manipulatives and resources such as Math Learning Center's interactive Fractions or Number Line apps through which students can explore these relationships. Technology choices that are aligned with strong learning goals provide opportunities for students to develop conceptual understanding, whereas computational fluency games may only assess what students already know.

2. Use technology to support good teaching, rather than as an add-on to the lesson.

Planning lessons that integrate appropriate technology into the teaching of math is more impactful and equitable than including technology only if there's time, or for students who finish early.

Technology that is made available "only if there's time" is not truly integrated into the lesson, and is likely to go unused by many students. Time may be teachers' most precious resource, and few teachers have time to spare during the school day. Why then plan for technology use that is unlikely to occur? The time that teachers spend bookmarking sites, distributing devices, or managing resources for "add-on" technology use could be better spent engaging all students in meaningful learning opportunities. Furthermore, when technology is positioned as a privilege for some students, its true value as a teaching and learning resource is undermined. (Imagine if textbooks or whiteboards were available only to students who met behavioral goals or finished their work early.) A more powerful and equitable use of technology resources is in the planning and enactment of the actual math lesson. If the selected technology assesses students' math skills, why not incorporate it in lieu of an exit ticket or quiz during the lesson? Rather than adding an opportunity to explore with an applet or virtual manipulative at the end of the lesson, why not build those in while students are learning new concepts? Instead of using a video or webpage to show early finishers how the math in your lesson might apply in "real life," why not capture all students' interest by launching the lesson with that same video or resource?

3. Leverage the novelty of technology to illuminate, not hide the math students are learning.

Elaborate graphics, sound effects, and gaming contexts may be appealing, but ask yourself: "Is this helping students to engage and learn, or is it tricking them into something they may not recognize as math later on?"

In 1978, an Apple II personal computer promotional brochure featured the phrase, "Simplicity is the ultimate sophistication," a precursor to the minimalist aesthetic that would become synonymous with the tech giant. This "less is more" idea can also be a useful consideration for integrating technology into your classroom. Although cute cartoon characters and silly noises might be fun features of a website or app, does it help children learn math? Not unless they are paired with math-rich experiences that align with how children learn. No matter the bells and whistles, using technology for drilling facts is typically little more than a high-tech replacement for flash cards. If this approach helps capture the attention of students who otherwise would hesitate to engage in practice, it may be useful. But practicing known facts is but a small component of learning math. On the other hand, tools such as screencasting (e.g., Screencastomatic, Explain Everything, Educreations, ShowMe) provide a blank slate where users can write, capture images, and record audio to reveal student thinking. Though these tools offer less novelty at first glance, they enable teachers and students to communicate representations, strategies, and thinking in ways that can be transformative in a math classroom. In general, select technology resources not for how they look, but for what they can do in support of math teaching and learning!

Connecting Cases with Standards

In this chapter, the case of Ms. Vaughan illustrates many opportunities for effective math teaching with technology: how the lesson aligns with Common Core State Standards for Mathematics in terms of both content and practices, and alignment with ISTE Standards for Students and for Educators. It may be useful to discuss and consider how the case aligns with math standards in your state or district, as well as ISTE Standards for Administrators and for Coaches.

Math Content Standard

CCSS.MATH.CONTENT.2.NBT.B.5 Fluently add and subtract within 100 using strategies based on place value, properties of operations, and/or the relationship between addition and subtraction.

Math Practice Standards

- Make sense of problems and persevere in solving them
- Reason abstractly and quantitatively

- Construct viable arguments and critique the reasoning of others

- Use appropriate tools strategically

- Attend to precision

ISTE Standards for Educators

5b. Design authentic learning activities that align with content area standards and use digital tools and resources to maximize active, deep learning.

6c. Create learning opportunities that challenge students to use a design process and computational thinking to innovate and solve problems.

7a. Provide alternative ways for students to demonstrate competency and reflect on their learning using technology.

ISTE Standards for Students

5c. Students break problems into component parts, extract key information, and develop descriptive models to understand complex systems or facilitate problem-solving.

6c. Students communicate complex ideas clearly and effectively by creating or using a variety of digital objects such as visualizations, models or simulations.

MOVING FROM INDIVIDUALIZED INSTRUCTION TO TECHNOLOGY FOR COLLABORATIVE LEARNING

Instead of using screens to enable disconnected, individualized learning, what if we leveraged technology to facilitate mathematical discourse and collaboration?

THIS CHAPTER INCLUDES two cases that illustrate teaching fraction equivalence with technology tools in third grade. As you read each of the following cases, consider how and what math is being taught, how technology is being used, and how those two ideas connect. After reading and reflecting on the two cases, compare your insights and connections with what research has to say about two big ideas illustrated in the cases: *Technology as a Collaborative Tool* and *Teaching Practices that Support Mathematical Learning.* You might also take a moment to examine how each of the lessons align with standards for math content, math practices; and ISTE standards for students, educators, and coaches. Standards alignment is offered at the end of the chapter for your reference.

Technology as a Collaborative Tool

Technology can be used to connect, collaborate, and communicate among students and teachers. Indeed, collaboration and communication are consistently listed among digital age skills that educators wish to develop among students. Simultaneously, teachers and administrators face calls for more personalized learning, ranging from the ISTE Standard for Educators, *5a. Use technology to create, adapt and personalize learning experiences that foster independent learning and accommodate learner differences and needs,* to individualized learning programs marketed by tech companies. For teachers looking to address all of these goals, there may be perceived tension between using technology to collaborate and communicate and using technology to personalize learning. In a math classroom, how can students communicate and collaborate if each student is working individually at their own pace? How can a teacher encourage mathematical discourse if each student is at a different place in a unit facilitated by a personalized learning program? Reconciling these tensions is an essential component of utilizing technology in a way that supports students' individual needs.

Teaching Practices that Support Math Learning

Well-known learning theorist Lev Vygotsky wrote, "What a child can do in cooperation today, s/he can do alone tomorrow." Teaching that encourages students to engage in math discussions not only supports cooperation and collaboration, but also provides children with opportunities to articulate and refine their reasoning through language and multimodal forms of communication. Classrooms rich in mathematical discourse support students' math learning by enabling them to collaboratively develop shared understanding. By honoring and discussing students' diverse contributions and ways of thinking, teachers can support learner differences and needs. Mathematical discourse communities can differentiate for students' individual needs by meeting other students where they are in their learning and leveraging partner, small-group, and whole-group interactions where they build upon the math that students know and can do. A focus on collaboration and communication in the classroom can also emphasize reasoning and concepts, rather than narrowly defining math in terms of right or wrong answers. Rather than isolating students to learn math at individual screens, technology can support classroom discourse communities that engage students in collaboration and math communication.

Ms. Anthony's third-grade class is learning about equivalent fractions. Consider how she integrates technology into the lesson, and her math teaching practices. How does she use technology to encourage communication and collaboration? To what extent does technology and instruction support personalized learning experiences that accommodate learner differences?

 **CASE 3.1**

Ms. Anthony's Grade 3 Fraction Equivalence Lesson

OBJECTIVES
- Recognize equivalent fractions using a variety of representations.

Ms. Anthony's classroom has 1:1 computers. Her school has recently begun to encourage more personalized learning experiences using classroom technology and free, online open educational resources. The goal of this initiative is to improve students' performance on state assessments through more individualized learning experiences using technology. This aligns with Ms. Anthony's goal of designing instruction that meets her students' diverse needs and strengths.

To implement personalized learning in her classroom, Ms. Anthony and her students use Khan Academy. Through their free, online resources, she is able to set up her class; assign lessons, videos, exercises, and quizzes; and view students' progress and scores. She enjoys that the online resources save time she would spend on grading, but realizes that she spends a similar amount of time setting up and monitoring the online class and data.

Since implementing personalized learning in her classroom, one of the challenges Ms. Anthony has faced is pacing. There is tension between meeting the district's scope-and-sequence with their adopted curriculum while also allowing students to learn at their own pace in the online environment. She addresses this by starting each unit with some lessons from the textbook, then gives students several days to work at their own pace to complete online lessons that are comparable to what is in her curriculum materials. A few days before the end of each unit, Ms. Anthony reviews and reteaches using lessons from the textbook. Then her students take the district's unit assessments.

Lately, Ms. Anthony's class has been learning about fractions, and will now be learning about equivalent fractions. Together as a whole group, Ms. Anthony shows students the first Khan Academy video in the Equivalent Fractions lesson. She answers student questions. After watching the video together, students may rewatch the video, proceed to new videos in the lesson, complete the exercises, or proceed to the next lesson about equivalent fractions on the number line. Students work online at their own pace until they have taken the online quiz for these two lessons. The videos, practice exercises, and quiz include finding equivalent fractions using numerals, bar models, area models of various shapes, and number lines. Exercises are numerical or selected-response.

Some students finish both lessons and the quiz in one day. For these students, Ms. Anthony assigns enrichment work from the textbook or allows them to play online math games from a class website. Other students are still trying to earn a passing quiz score at the end of the second day. As students work online during class, Ms. Anthony spends some of her time assisting those who are struggling. Other times, she monitors students as they work individually, making sure they are on-task. When she is not working with individual students or monitoring the classroom, she often checks student progress through the data available to her online.

Ms. Anthony is happy to be contributing to the vision of more personalized learning in her school, but has some mixed feelings about how it is going. She hasn't noticed a major difference in unit test scores as compared to her grade-level team members who aren't using personalized learning in their classrooms. But she does have data that shows her students are progressing through the lessons. She has noticed that the classroom is generally quieter during math now, but that there is less opportunity for partner and group work, which she believes is important. Some students have had a more difficult time sitting still lately, and some parents have also communicated concerns about increased screen time for their children. Ms. Anthony is excited about how she and her students are using technology for learning math, but continues to reflect on the right balance between personalized learning, her school's math curriculum, and her teaching philosophy that will best meet her students' diverse needs.

Reflection Questions

Consider Ms. Anthony's use of technology in this lesson. Based on her perception of students' needs and district preferences, she selected a technology that aligned with the math content she needed to teach.

- Would you consider this a technology-rich lesson? Why or why not?

- What was the purpose of Ms. Anthony's technology use in this lesson?

- How did Ms. Anthony's integration of technology advance the teaching and learning of math in this lesson?

- What were she and/or the students able to do with technology that was different from or better than what could have been done without the technology?

- Might the use of technology in this lesson hinder students' math learning in any way? Why or why not?

Next, consider the math teaching practices in Ms. Anthony's lesson.

- What were Ms. Anthony's goals for this math lesson?

- How did she address students' individual needs in this lesson?

- Would you describe this lesson as more teacher-centered, or more student-centered? Why?

- To what extent did students have equitable access to learn and demonstrate their understanding in this lesson?

- Overall, what strengths do you see in this lesson? What opportunities do you notice?

●●●●

Ms. Gonzales's third-grade class is also learning about equivalent fractions. As you read about Ms. Gonzales's lesson, consider how she integrates technology into the lesson and her math teaching practices. How does she use technology to encourage communication and collaboration? To what extent does technology and instruction support personalized learning experiences that accommodate learner differences?

CASE 3.2
Ms. Gonzales's Grade 3 Fraction Equivalence Lesson

OBJECTIVES
- Recognize equivalent fractions using a variety of fraction representations.

At the beginning of the lesson, Ms. Gonzales pairs students with a shoulder partner, and asks one student from each pair to get a laptop from a cart in the back of the room. Students will work with partners on the laptops throughout the lesson. While students are getting their computers, she projects an image of different representations of one-third (Figure 3.1) using the Fractions app from the Math Learning Center (apps.mathlearningcenter.org/fractions).

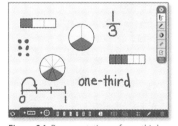
Figure 3.1 Representations of one-third.

Ms. Gonzales asks students to discuss which representations do *not* show a fraction equivalent to one-third. After about a minute of partner discussions, she points at each of the representations and asks students whether or not they think it is equivalent to one-third. Some students disagree about whether the circle model with three of the nine sections shaded is equivalent to one-third, instead representing it as three-ninths. Ms. Gonzales facilitates a brief discussion during which peers justify why three-ninths is equivalent to one-third. A similar conversation occurs regarding the set model of two red dots and four blue dots, after two students contend that it shows two-fourths, others say it is two-sixths, and others contend that two-sixths is the same as one-third. Students agree that the fraction bar showing three shaded out of six total sections is not equivalent to one-third.

After this introductory exercise, Ms. Gonzales asks students to access the Desmos Classroom Activity she created by going to student.desmos.com. On her screen, she displays the class code that students need to gain access to the activity. As students log in, she explains that today they will be working with a partner to do an online card sort. She displays the screen that students see on their laptops (see Figure 3.2) and tells them to work together to sort the cards into groups of equivalent fraction amounts. The card sort includes three different fraction amounts (one-half, two-thirds, and three-quarters), and equivalent forms shown in numeric and word forms, fraction bar models, fraction circle models, number lines, and set models.

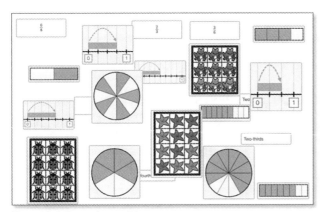

Figure 3.2 Online card sort activity.

Students spend the next several minutes working together with their partners to sort the cards into groups that represent equivalent fraction amounts. (Within Desmos, cards can be sorted into groups with drag and drop motions.) Meanwhile, Ms. Gonzales walks around the room listening to student discussions and periodically looking at her own computer where she can view students' Desmos screens. She anticipates that some students might incorrectly sort by representation, and other students might only match representations for the same fractions, but not forms of equivalent fractions (e.g., one-half and one-half, but not one-half and two-fourths). Viewing students' work through teacher.desmos.com enables her to purposefully select and sequence which pairs' work she will display so that the class can engage in a whole-group discussion. She quietly asks selected student pairs if they will be willing to explain and discuss their work, and all agree to do so.

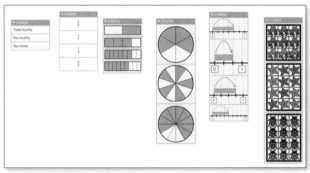

Figure 3.3 Pete and Brooke's card sort.

As students finish, she asks the class to close their laptops so they can discuss the card sort. Ms. Gonzales begins the whole-group discussion by displaying Pete and Brooke's work (shown in Figure 3.3) and asking why their sort makes sense.

Several students raise their hands. She calls on Eleanor who says that Pete and Brooke sorted the cards into the type of picture. Ms. Gonzales answers, "Yes, the board shows the cards sorted by the type of representation: words, numbers, fraction bars, fraction circles, number lines, and sets. Each group has the same kind of representations, but do the groups show equivalent fractions?" Brooke realizes their error and replies, "No. The fractions in each group aren't the same because the pictures don't show the same amounts." Ms. Gonzales affirms Brooke's response. She points to the fraction bars as an example of fractional amounts that are not all equivalent to one another.

Next, Ms. Gonzales displays Angelia and Emelda's work (shown in Figure 3.4) on the board for students to discuss:

She asks Angelia and Emelda to explain their sort to the rest of the class. The two explain how they figured out a fraction for each card, and then matched the ones that were identical. They ended up with seven different matches: one-half, four-sixths, two-thirds, six-eighths, nine-twelfths, three-quarters, and six-ninths. They found no matches for the following fractions: three-sixths, five-tenths, two-fourths, four-eighths, and six-twelfths. Ms. Gonzales suggests, "Let's have Aubrey and Gabriel explain how they sorted the cards and see how that compares to what Angelia and Emelda just showed us." She asks the next pair to explain as she displays their sort (shown in Figure 3.5) via the projector.

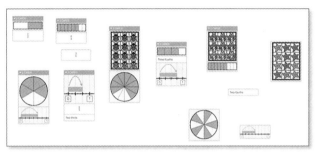

Figure 3.4 Angelia and Emelda's card sort

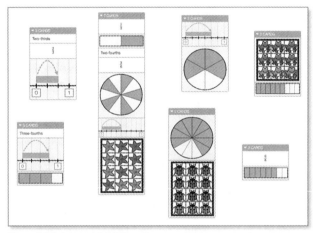

Figure 3.5 Aubrey and Gabriel's card sort.

Aubrey and Gabriel go to the front of the classroom and point at the cards as they explain their choices to the class. Like Angelia and Emelda, they also sorted cards into seven categories: one-half, four-sixths, two-thirds, six-eighths, nine-twelfths, three-quarters, and six-ninths. But they did not have any cards left over. Instead, they realized that three-sixths, five-tenths, two-fourths, four-eighths, and six-twelfths are equivalent to one-half and placed those cards in one category. When Ms. Gonzales asks why, Aubrey justifies their choice, "Because we knew that all of those fractions are the same as one-half, we put them all in one big category."

"Hmmm, one big category for one-half … Walker and Dominick, you had seven categories in your sort too. Tell us what you think about Gabriel's idea of making one big category out of all the fractions equivalent to one-half," Ms. Gonzales asks as she displays the next pair's work on the board, as shown in Figure 3.6.

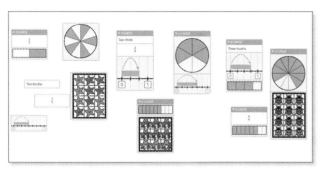

Figure 3.6 Walker and Dominick's card sort.

"We matched up seven fractions, but we also sort of put them in bigger groups too," explains Dominick. "So instead of putting them all completely together like Aubrey and Gabriel did, we matched the two fractions that showed one-half, and then we put all of the other fractions that aren't one-half but are equal to one-half next to that group."

Ms. Gonzales says, "Oh, ok. So what Dominick and Walker did was match the fractions they thought were equal, and then put other equivalent fractions near that category. Did you do that with fractions other than one-half?"

Walker points to the images on the board as he elaborates. "Yeah. We made categories for two-thirds, and four-sixths, and six-ninths, but then we figured out that those are all kind of the same so we put those categories all together in the middle here. Then we did the same thing for everything that was equal to three-fourths."

Ms. Gonzales invites all students to discuss with their partner whether they agree or disagree with Walker's ideas about which fractions are equivalent. After a couple of minutes, she invites Amber to share what she and her partner have discussed.

"We agreed with Walker and Dominick, because if you compare the bar models for three-fourths and six-ninths, you can see that the same amount is shaded and they are the same."

"Jerald, I heard you and your partner explain it a different way. Could you share that with the class?" asks Ms. Gonzales.

Jerald responds, "We looked at the red and blue pictures and with the frogs. Even though there are six red frogs and three blue frogs, which is six-ninths, you can also look at the rows. Two of the three rows of frogs are red, so you could just write two-thirds instead."

"Ok class, thumbs up if you agree with Amber and Gerald's explanations." Nearly all students raise their thumbs in response to Ms. Gonzales's prompt. However, she knows from monitoring students' work and discussions that not all students completely understand fraction equivalence yet. She will provide additional supports for these students during the next activity in this lesson. Before concluding the group discussion, she invites one last group to share their work (Figure 3.7), now projected on the board. "Jacqueline and Alonzo, you sorted all of the cards into only three categories. Please talk to us about your work."

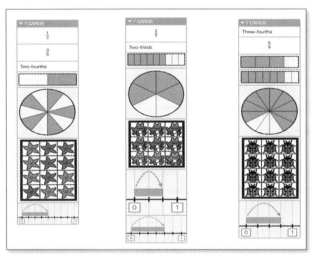

Figure 3.7 Jacqueline and Alonzo's card sort.

Alonzo begins by saying that he and Jacqueline knew that one-half, three-sixths, and two-fourths are all equivalent, and that the bar model showed one-half. He then explains that the circle shows five out of ten shaded sections, that six starfish are red and six blue, so that shows half, and the number line shows four-eighths, which is also equivalent to one-half. He refers to previously presented work, "We sorted them just like Walker and Dominick, only we connected all of the fractions that were equal to one another into big groups: one-half, two-thirds, and three-fourths."

After the whole-group discussion, Ms. Gonzales directs students toward a bookmarked Khan Academy lesson about equivalent fractions. Based on her observations of student work and explanations during the whole-group discussion, she directs some student pairs to view videos about equivalent fractions and equivalent fractions on number lines. For student pairs who seemed to mostly understand during whole-group discussion, she encourages them to work on practice exercises, noting where they can click for help if they're stuck. She invites student pairs who seemed to have mastered the content during whole-group discussion to proceed to the Khan Academy quiz. Ms. Gonzales monitors data on students' progress from her teacher data display on Khan Academy.

When students successfully finish the online exercises and quiz, Ms. Gonzales directs them to Equivalent Fractions, an online interactive resource from the National Council of Teachers of Mathematics, and briefly models how the game works. Using the automatic mode, the screen displays a fraction using a square or circle model, as well as a number line. Students can then use sliders to generate two equivalent fractions (shown as square or circle models, depending on the option students choose). The equivalent fractions are shown on the number line and can be checked. When they are finished, the students' symbolic representations are automatically recorded in a table.

Ms. Gonzales asks each partner to take turns generating equivalent fractions using the Equivalent Fractions interactive resource. Students explore and practice together until Ms. Gonzales gives a one-minute warning to wrap up the problem they are on, and to leave their screens as-is.

To wrap up the lesson, Ms. Gonzales asks three pairs to share the equivalent fractions they found in the interactive resource. She records the equivalent fractions on the board for all students to see. As an exit ticket, she asks students to individually write down one of the fractions on the board and draw a different representation of an equivalent fraction.

Reflection Questions

Consider Ms. Gonzales's use of technology in this lesson. As you reflect and discuss, consider what happened in Ms. Gonzales's lesson, and how it compares with Ms. Anthony's class.

- Would you consider this a technology-rich lesson? Why or why not?

- What was the purpose of Ms. Gonzales's technology use in this lesson?

- How did Ms. Gonzales's integration of technology advance the teaching and learning of math in this lesson?

- What were the teacher and/or the students able to do with technology that was different from or better than what could have been done without technology?

- Might the use of technology in this lesson hinder students' math learning in any way? Why or why not?

Next, consider the math teaching practices in Ms. Gonzales's lesson and how they compare with the practices in the first scenario.

- What were Ms. Gonzales's goals for this math lesson?

- How did she address students' individual needs in this lesson?

- Would you describe this lesson as more teacher-centered or more student-centered? Why?

- To what extent did students have equitable access to learn and demonstrate their understanding in this lesson?

- Overall, what strengths do you see in this lesson? What opportunities do you notice?

● ● ● ●

What Does the Research Say?

The following research findings support the use of technology as a collaborative tool:

- Technology enables networking, communicating, and collaborating in increasingly sophisticated ways. In a digitally connected world, students across the classroom, or across the world, can communicate and work collaboratively in real-time. Decades of research has shown that student engagement in collaborative, connected learning environments can positively impact their motivation, conceptual understanding, and perseverance for solving challenging problems. This has been shown as particularly impactful for struggling learners. Furthermore, studies involving collaborative interactions with technology have shown more equitable participation than what often occurs in classroom discussions absent of technology. (See, for instance, Beatty & Geiger, 2009; Goos, Galbraith, Renshaw, & Geiger, 2000; Hoadley, Hsi, & Berman, 1995; Hsi & Hoadley, 1997; Hurme & Jarvela, 2005; Riel, 1991; Roschelle et al., 2010; Scardamalia & Bereiter, 1993; Suthers, Toth, & Weiner, 1997; White, 2006).

- Use of technology as a collaborative tool aligns with prevailing learning theories in math education. Whereas technology-enabled, personalized learning approaches overwhelmingly employ behaviorist approaches to teaching and learning math (Dishon, 2017), math education research has, for decades, emphasized and drawn upon constructivist and sociocultural theories (Cobb, 1994) for supporting more equitable student learning through collaborative, inquiry-driven, and discourse-rich teaching approaches. Using technology as a collaborative tool aligns with theory and research in math education. Using technology to personalize learning with behaviorist approaches that do not afford collaboration and communication can disregard decades of research in teaching and learning math.

- When students spend a significant amount of class time engaged individually with technology, mathematical discussion in the classroom can decrease (Thomas, 2013). However, the opposite can be true when students engage in models of personalized learning that include opportunities to work collaboratively with peers. Technology can impact the nature of human interactions and the interactions among learners, teachers, mathematical knowledge, and learning contexts (Borba et al., 2016). Plainly stated, using technology as a collaborative tool while also promoting personalized learning goals is a complex endeavor for math teachers.

Following are some math teaching practices that support student learning:

- In developing a framework of high-leverage, effective math teaching practices, the National Council of Teachers of Mathematics (2014) highlights research-based principles of learning including: "Learners should have experiences that enable them to construct knowledge socially, through discourse, activity, and interaction related to meaningful problems" (p. 9). A body of research, conducted over decades, continues to emphasize the importance of discourse and social knowledge construction for learning math.

- Mathematical discourse includes focused classroom discussion about mathematical ideas, as well as other forms of communication. Mathematical discourse enables students to develop understanding through constructing, sharing, critiquing, clarifying, and refining their own ideas, and those of others. The multimodal nature of mathematical discourse opens possibilities for technology to support this important component of learning math.

- Researchers have identified a number of strategies to support and facilitate meaningful mathematical discourse in classrooms. The five practices for orchestrating classroom discussions (Smith & Stein, 2011) suggest that teachers in whole-class contexts anticipate possible student thinking before a lesson, monitor students' mathematical work, select specific students to present their work in a particular sequence, and connect across student work to highlight the math they want students to learn. Math talk moves (Chapin, O'Connor, & Anderson, 2013) offer another strategy for engaging students in partner, small-group, and whole-group discussions about mathematics.

- In contrast to teaching and learning through mathematical discourse in collaborative contexts, individualized instruction is an approach that typically draws from a behaviorist approach to learning. A classic case study in mathematics education (Erlwanger, 1973) highlights a sixth-grade student, Benny, who used an individualized curriculum in the 1970s. The goal was, "… 'to develop an educational program which is maximally adaptive to the requirements of the individual' Lindvall & Cox, 1970, p. 34)" (p. 88). Although Benny performed well within the (non technological) program, researchers revealed a number of misunderstandings and error patterns in his mathematical conception of rules and answers. The role of discussion, or lack thereof, is described in the study: "There is never any reason for Benny to participate in a discussion with either his teachers or his peers about what he has learned, and what his views are about mathematics. Nevertheless, Benny has his own views about mathematics—its rules and its answers" (Erlwanger, 1973, p. 52). As teachers grapple with incorporating technology-enabled, personalized learning programs in modern classrooms, this seminal study offers a precautionary tale about individualized math instruction and the need to balance discourse about concepts with practice of procedures.

Reflecting on Technology in Math Teaching

As you read the cases of Ms. Anthony's and Ms. Gonzales's third-grade classrooms, you should have noticed significant differences in how the math was taught, and how technology was used to support math teaching. In Ms. Anthony's class, she aligned her technology use with a math goal of identifying equivalent fractions using various representations, and a technology goal of more personalized learning to meet students' individual needs. Ms. Gonzales aligned her technology use with the same content goal, but used technology to facilitate collaboration and discourse to meet and leverage students' individualized needs and assets. In both cases, we see evidence of alignment between goals and use of technology for teaching and learning math. Ms. Anthony has embraced a technology goal for personalized learning, but acknowledges some concerns that are resulting from that approach. The way she is using technology for personalized learning does not necessarily align with what research tells us about the nature of learning math. This helps to illustrate that aligning technology use with content goals and technology-use initiatives is important, but tensions can arise when technology use conflicts with what research and theory tell us about teaching and learning math (with or without technology). Table 3.1 compares the cases of Ms. Anthony and Ms. Gonzales.

TABLE 3.1 Use of Technology in the Cases of Ms. Anthony and Ms. Gonzales

	The Case of Ms. Anthony	The Case of Ms. Gonzales
What technology is used?	1:1 laptops; online personalized lessons, videos, exercises, and quiz from Khan Academy	Virtual fraction manipulative; online card sort through Desmos; online videos, exercises and quiz from Khan Academy; Equivalent Fractions via online interactive resource from NCTM
What math is emphasized?	Identifying equivalent fractions using numerals, area models of various shapes, bar models, and number lines.	Identifying equivalent fractions using numerals, words, circle area models, bar models, set models, and number lines.
How is the lesson launched?	Ms. Anthony shows a demonstrative video at the beginning of the first class, and then students work independently to progress through two lessons and a quiz.	Ms. Gonzales uses a virtual manipulative to display a variety of fraction representations, and uses partner talk and class discussion to launch a discussion about equivalent fractions.
Who is doing the math in this lesson?	Students watch videos that explain equivalent fractions, and then complete practice questions and quizzes individually.	Students work with a partner to sort equivalent fraction representations in a digital environment, complete Khan Academy online exercises, and work with a partner to create equivalent fractions using an online interactive resource.
When and how is technology used in the lesson?	The lesson is almost completely conveyed through personalized learning technology.	Ms. Gonzales uses technology to launch the lesson, facilitate student collaboration and discussion through an online card sort, assess students as they work together, and support students as they create equivalent fractions online at the end of the lesson.

A helpful lens for considering Ms. Anthony's and Ms. Gonzales's technology use in these lessons might be to ask, *"How does the use of technology in this lesson align with effective math teaching practices?"* Because her math lesson relies on technology-enabled pedagogy that runs counter to research and best practices for teaching and learning math, it is not surprising that Ms. Anthony has mixed feelings about the outcomes of her approach.

It is also important to consider the role technology plays in providing equitable access to learning math. Ms. Anthony was motivated, in part, to use technology-enabled personalized learning to meet individualized student needs. To some extent, students could work at their own pace (within the constraints of her scope and sequence), and the arrangement allowed her more time to individually assist students who were struggling. However, she noticed that some of her students had more difficulty focusing during individual computer-based learning, suggesting that the approach was not the same with all students. Although the approach enabled some individualized pacing, all students ended up doing the same work in more or less the same way. On the other hand, students in Ms. Gonzales's classroom used technology collaboratively throughout the lesson. Students worked together to complete a sorting activity online, and then Ms. Gonzales facilitated a classroom discussion based on their technology-enabled work. Even though some student contributions weren't completely correct, Ms. Gonzales leveraged all student contributions to highlight important student thinking about equivalent fractions. For reinforcement and assessment, she asked the students to complete online practice and assessment exercises, differentiating the online assignments according to what she observed during whole-group discussion. Throughout the lesson, all students had an opportunity to use the same technologies in ways that support collaboration and communication about equivalent fractions.

Recommendations for Practice

This chapter began with the question: *Instead of using screens to enable disconnected individualized learning, what if we leverage technology to facilitate math discourse and collaboration?* Vignettes from Ms. Anthony's and Ms. Gonzales's classrooms show contrasting visions of what these two ideas could look like in elementary classrooms. How can you leverage technology to facilitate math discourse and collaboration? Here are three suggestions with accompanying elaboration and examples.

1. Make sure students have a chance to engage in math discourse during every lesson. Technology should support communication and collaboration, not replace it.

Giving students an opportunity to communicate mathematically lets them know that their ideas are worth sharing. A variety of technologies can support sharing. In this case, the teacher used Desmos to facilitate a card sort, and facilitated a math discussion around student responses. The technology allowed her to easily view all student responses and to select, sequence, and display student work for discussion. Tools such as Pear Deck and Near Pod can elicit student work, and allow the teacher to display student contributions for class discussion.

Teachers can also use technology to facilitate mathematical communication in non verbal formats. Through tools such as Google Classroom, Edmodo, or classroom blogs, students can share pictures or written accounts of their mathematical reasoning. Asking students to examine, discuss, or comment on one another's contributions supports the Common Core mathematical practice, MP3: *Viable arguments are constructed and the reasoning of others is critiqued.*

2. Technology can, and should, support effective teaching practices, but technology won't replace the teacher!

Fill in the blank: "_____ today not only rivals formal education, but better yet, it increasingly is being used to supplement the work of the teacher." Did you guess internet? Computers? Maybe even television? This is the opening sentence of an article entitled, "Radio in the Classroom" from 1942! The tension between technology and teacher in the classroom is nearly a century old, but technology has yet to replace teachers.

Technology can change the role of teachers and students. In this chapter, the two vignettes showed how Khan Academy could be used in different ways to support different teacher and student roles. The same could be said of tools such as IXL or DreamBox learning. Technologies that offer personalized experiences for learners can supplement good classroom instruction without supplanting the teacher. Regardless of which technology a teacher chooses to use, it is important to evaluate how it fits with your teaching practices and reflects classroom roles. If your teaching is guided by constructivist or sociocultural learning theories, consider whether the way you're using technology aligns with your priorities. If students are staring at isolated screens in a direct transmission model of learning math, reconsider what and how students are expected to learn math.

3. Use technology to facilitate a variety of collaboration structures.

In some contexts, sharing technology is necessary due to limited device availability. In other situations, students have access to 1:1 devices. Whether students share devices or have their own, technology can be employed in ways that promote collaboration. Tools such as connected whiteboard apps or G Suite collaborative apps (Docs, Sheets, Slides) enable real-time collaboration on written or visual projects. In an elementary math classroom, students can use digital collaborative spaces to type out their thinking (in developmentally appropriate language), or create presentations of their work to share with the class.

Students can also collaborate with partners on shared devices. Working together to solve a card sort in Desmos, or represent a math problem using a virtual manipulative requires both cooperation and communication. Teachers can use videos to pose interesting problems to groups of students who then work collaboratively to find solutions. Three-act tasks from gfletchy.com or Dan Meyer (blog.mrmeyer.com) leverage technology to pose questions that do not require individual devices, but invite collaboration and mathematical discussion. Using technology (interactive whiteboard, projector, screencasts) to select and display student work with interesting tasks can also encourage collaboration and mathematical discussion.

Connecting Cases with Standards

In this chapter, the cases of Ms. Anthony and Ms. Gonzales demonstrate ways in which technology can be used to teach a Grade 3 lesson on equivalent fractions. Below, find alignment with Common Core State Standards for mathematics, as well as ISTE Standards for Students and for Educators. It may be useful for you to discuss and consider how the case aligns with math standards in your state or district, as well as ISTE Standards for Administrators and for Coaches.

Math Content Standards

> **CCSS.MATH.CONTENT.3.NF.3** Explain equivalence of fractions in special cases, and compare fractions by reasoning about their size.

> **CCSS.MATH.CONTENT.3.NF.A.3.A** Understand two fractions as equivalent (equal) if they are the same size, or the same point on a number line.

CCSS.MATH.CONTENT.3.NF.A.3.B Recognize and generate simple equivalent fractions, (e.g., one-half = two-fourths, four-sixths = two-thirds). Explain why the fractions are equivalent, (e.g., by using a visual fraction model).

Math Practice Standards

- Make sense of problems and persevere in solving them

- Reason abstractly and quantitatively

- Construct viable arguments and critique the reasoning of others

- Attend to precision

ISTE Standards for Educators

5a. Use technologies to create, adapt and personalize learning experiences that foster independent learning and accommodate learner differences and needs.

5b. Design authentic learning activities that align with content area standards and use digital tools and resources to maximize active, deep learning.

6a. Foster a culture where students take ownership of their learning goals and outcomes in both independent and group settings.

6b. Manage the use of technology and student learning strategies in digital platforms, virtual environments, hands-on makerspaces or in the field.

7b. Use technology to design and implement a variety of formative and summative assessments that accommodate learner needs, provide timely feedback to students and inform instruction.

7c. Use assessment data to guide progress and communicate with students, parents and education stakeholders to build student self-direction.

ISTE Standards for Students

1c. Students use technology to seek feedback that informs and improves their practice and to demonstrate their learning in a variety of ways.

4d. Students exhibit a tolerance for ambiguity, perseverance and the capacity to work with open-ended problems.

MOVING FROM ASSESSING
WHAT STUDENTS KNOW TO ELICITING
HOW STUDENTS UNDERSTAND

● Instead of using technology as a tool for assessment *of*
● math learning, what if we leverage technology as a tool
● to assess *for* learning?

THIS CHAPTER describes two kindergarten classes where students are learning about shapes. Both cases include technology in the lessons; note how the use of technology supports the teaching of math. At the beginning of each case, take a look at the ISTE Standards and math standards in your state to see how the two cases align with these expectations; later you can compare with the alignment at the end of the chapter. Once you have read and reflected on the two cases, read what research has to say about two big ideas: *Technology as an Assessment Tool* and *Leveraging Students' Mathematical Understanding;* consider how that connects with what you noticed. Finally, consider the recommendations for practice as you connect the research and the case studies with your own classroom.

Technology as an Assessment Tool

The U.S. Department of Education's Office of Educational Technology sets the goal: *At all levels, our education system will leverage the power of technology to measure what matters and use assessment data to improve learning.* Assessment helps us measure and respond to what students do and do not understand. Technology can allow us to do so more efficiently. From the early days of Scantron machines that enabled quick scoring of multiple-choice assessment items to computerized adaptive assessment, technology continues to provide increasingly sophisticated assessment tools. Many online programs now offer instantaneous feedback for students and voluminous amounts of assessment data on teacher dashboards. Although these summative measures can be helpful for many purposes, it is also important to acknowledge the potential of technology to formatively assess students to inform more in-the-moment decision-making. Using technology can reveal more nuanced information about how students understand math, enabling more responsive teaching and meaningful learning.

Leveraging Students' Mathematical Understanding

Assessment is more than grading how many answers students get right and wrong. Good classroom assessment practices elicit students' mathematical understanding—math they know and how they know it. Posing questions that elicit common misconceptions or reasoning strategies and providing students with opportunities to demonstrate their understanding in a variety of ways allows teachers better access to interpret and leverage student thinking. Technology can be a useful tool for making student thinking more visible. Once teachers have a better sense of what students know, they can adapt math instruction to more equitably improve learning.

Mr. Evers's kindergarten class is learning to identify two-dimensional shapes. He integrates technology into the lesson as a way to assess student work. As you read the following case, consider the effectiveness of technology and assessment practices during the lesson.

 CASE 4.1

Mr. Evers's Kindergarten Identifying Shapes Lesson

OBJECTIVES

- Recognize equivalent fractions using a variety of representations.

Mr. Evers is teaching a lesson about shape identification to his kindergarten class. He knows that some kids already know most, or all, of the shape names. His challenge will be to keep those kids engaged in a lesson that also addresses the needs of students who are still learning shapes and shape names. He decides to use an online video to introduce shapes and shape names. The video includes a song and game in which a shape is displayed on the screen. The name of the shape is stated out loud and written on the screen. Students sing and dance along to a shape name game/song. The shapes in the video include circle, triangle, rectangle, square, oval, and rhombus.

After the shape sing- and dance-along, Mr. Evers projects the Pattern Shapes virtual manipulative from Math Learning Center (apps.mathlearningcenter.org/pattern-shapes) from his iPad onto the whiteboard. He chooses an outline of a turtle for students to fill in using pattern block shapes, as shown in Figure 4.1.

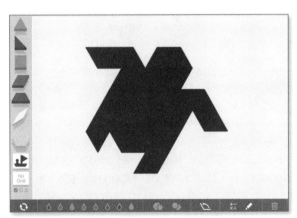

Figure 4.1 Pattern block turtle outline.

He chooses sticks with students' names to randomly call on students. Students take turns going to the iPad, dragging one shape, and placing it onto the turtle. With each shape, Mr. Evers asks the class to identify the name of the shape. Because it was not in the video, he tells students that the red shape is called a trapezoid. Eventually, the class fills in the turtle shape with a variety of pattern blocks (shown in Figure 4.2).

Figure 4.2 Completed pattern block turtle.

Mr. Evers divides students into three groups and finishes the class with station rotations. He wants to assess how well students can identify shapes on their own. In one station, students work on class computers to complete the online IXL Kindergarten skill assessment, Name the two-dimensional shape (ixl.com/math/kindergarten/name-the-two-dimensional-shape). Once logged in (a previously-developed routine in the classroom), students can read the words on the screen or press the speaker to hear the directions, as shown in Figure 4.3.

The website gives students immediate feedback as to the correctness of their answers. It keeps track of the number of questions answered, time elapsed, and a score. Mr. Evers can refer back to the assessment data to get a sense of students' progress in the lesson. While a third of the students take online assessments, another third work at their desks coloring shapes and tracing the names of each shape on a workbook page. The rest of the students use physical pattern blocks to trace shapes and draw a picture. All students have an opportunity to rotate to each of the three stations. This approach keeps students engaged and enables Mr. Evers to use online individual assessment, even though he only has a few classroom computers. When he reviews the assessment data, he's happy to see that students performed very well at identifying shapes.

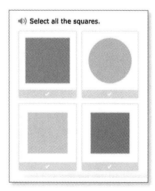

Figure 4.3 IXL shape question.

The next day, as a warm-up, Mr. Evers has students complete a workbook page on which they color various types of shapes in different colors. Because the assessment results from the previous day were quite positive, he is discouraged to see that many students are not correctly identifying some of the triangles, squares, and rectangles. He will spend time today reteaching about identifying shapes.

Reflection Questions

First consider Mr. Evers's use of technology in this lesson. He selected technologies to keep his students engaged in learning about his lesson objectives.

- Would you consider this a technology-rich lesson? Why or why not?

- What was the purpose of Mr. Evers's technology use in this lesson?

- How did Mr. Evers's integration of technology advance the teaching and learning of math in this lesson?

- What were he and/or the students able to do with technology that was different from or better than what could have been done without technology?

- How did Mr. Evers use technology as an assessment tool?

Now, consider the math teaching practices in Mr. Evers's lesson.

- What were Mr. Evers's math goals for this lesson?

- To what extent did students have equitable access to learn and demonstrate their understanding in this lesson?

- Overall, what strengths do you see in this lesson? What opportunities do you notice?

- How did Mr. Evers elicit and build upon students' mathematical thinking?

- Why do you think some students had trouble identifying triangles, squares, and rectangles, even though they performed well on the previous day's assessment?

●●●●

Ms. Jennings's kindergarten class is also learning about identifying shapes. As you read about Ms. Jennings's lesson, consider how she integrates technology into the lesson and her math teaching practices. How does she use technology as an assessment tool? To what extent does she leverage students' understanding to improve learning in the lesson?

+ CASE 4.2

Ms. Jennings's Kindergarten Identifying Shapes Lesson

OBJECTIVES

- Identify two-dimensional shapes.

Ms. Jennings's kindergarten class will be learning to identify shapes in today's class. Nearly all of her students can identify basic shapes such as circles and squares, but she expects other shapes to be new for most of the kids. Ms. Jennings has used Google Slides and Pear Deck to prepare an interactive slideshow. She will project her slides onto the whiteboard, and students will share iPads to interact with some of the slides she's prepared.

Students in Ms. Jennings's class are seated in pods, or desks placed in groups of four. At the beginning of class, she gives each group an iPad, preloaded with the activity she'll have them use during the lesson. The children are accustomed to using an iPad during class and, because there are only a limited number of devices, they are also accustomed to working cooperatively on the iPads. They have previously developed routines for accessing apps and logging in to frequently used programs.

She begins the class by showing a slide with four shapes. Ms. Jennings asks students to open their iPad and talk with others in their group about the names of the shapes they see. After a couple of minutes, she asks students to share their ideas about the shapes. All groups were able to accurately identify the square, rectangle, and triangle. Some students didn't know the name for the hexagon, or called it a "stop sign," or octagon, instead. She showed the names of each shape so students could see the shape, hear the spoken name of the shape, and see the written word (see Figure 4.4).

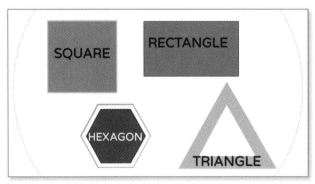

Figure 4.4 Four shapes.

Ms. Jennings points at the triangle and asks students how they know it is a triangle. Student responses include, "It has three sides," and, "It points up." She leads the class in counting the number of sides on the hexagon, showing that hexagons have six sides. She asks students to discuss the difference between a square and rectangle. Students conclude that both squares and rectangles have four sides and four corners. They notice that the square's sides are all the same size, but the rectangle has two long sides, and two short sides. Although these are not precise mathematical definitions, Ms. Jennings decides they are adequate working definitions at this level.

Ms. Jennings knows that young children sometimes have difficulty recognizing different versions of shapes. She knows this is relevant to her students because she just heard a student say a triangle "points up." To elicit and address these misconceptions, she shows the interactive slide shown in Figure 4.5, and asks students to circle all of the triangles and draw an X through all of the rectangles.

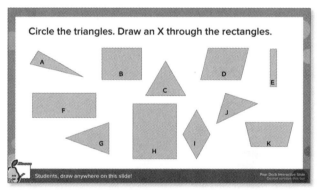

Figure 4.5 Identifying triangles and rectangles.

As expected, all student groups identify shape C as a triangle, and shape F as a rectangle. Few student groups identified shape A or J as triangles, or shape E as a rectangle. By drawing out these common misconceptions, Ms. Jennings is able to address them with the whole class. She advances to the next slide (shown in Figure 4.6), which links directly to the Pattern Shapes virtual manipulative from Math Learning Center (apps.mathlearningcenter.org/pattern-shapes). The students identify the pattern block shapes they recognize (triangles, square, hexagon). Ms. Jennings leads a discussion about triangles and squares. She writes the shape names and shows the corresponding pattern blocks. Students agree that even when she moves the shapes or makes them a different size, they are still triangles and squares. She then introduces two new shapes: rhombus and trapezoid.

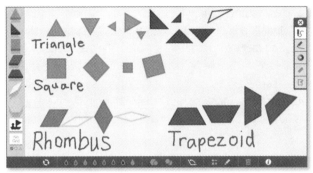

Figure 4.6 Identifying pattern block shapes.

To check for understanding, Ms. Jennings advances to the next slide (Figure 4.7), which is interactive. Student screens now show five shapes and five shape names. The directions for the slide are to draw lines between each shape and its corresponding name. Because the children are beginning readers, Ms. Jennings reminds them they can press the speaker to hear each word out loud.

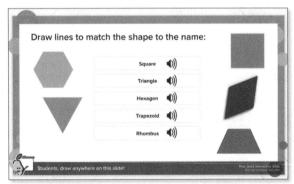

Figure 4.7 Matching pattern block images and shape names.

Ms. Jennings can see students' work on her screen and notices that several groups have confused trapezoid and rhombus, the two newest, least-familiar shapes for students. Before starting the next activity, they review the shape names again, starting with trapezoid and rhombus. Then, Ms. Jennings uses the Pattern Shapes app to model what it looks like to create a shape with pattern blocks, and then passes out sets of physical pattern blocks to each table. At this point, she wants students to work with the physical pattern blocks because they are easier for young children to manipulate.

She tells students to each create a picture with the blocks, and then tell their group members the names of the shapes they used. As she circulates around the room, she takes pictures of student work so she can recreate their pictures in the app and discuss as a whole class. She reproduces and projects Gwen's pattern block picture, (as shown in Figure 4.8). Ms. Jennings asks Gwen to tell the class about her picture.

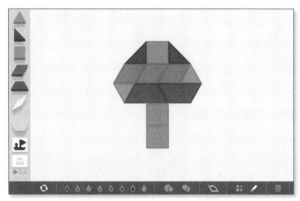

Figure 4.8 Gwen's pattern block tree.

Gwen explains, "I made a tree with the blocks." When asked about the shapes she used to make her tree, Gwen replies, "…with some help I used orange squares, green and purple triangles, blue rhombuses, and red trapezoids." Ms. Jennings points at shapes that are turned in different directions, reinforcing that their orientation does not change their shape.

After learning about shape names and exploring with the pattern blocks, Ms. Jennings concludes the lesson with a rotation activity. She divides the class into three groups. One group goes to a table in the back of the room to work directly with Ms. Jennings on creating shape drawings. This enables her to ask questions to individual students, and get a more in-depth sense of each student's understanding. Another group of students completes a workbook page on naming shapes. They color a shape and trace the name of the shape below it. The third group completes wooden shape puzzles. The fourth group works on the iPads to answer seven "Name Shape 3" practice exercises from Khan Academy. The exercises include squares, rectangles, hexagons, circles, rhombuses, triangles, and trapezoids—all in various orientations. Fortunately, Ms. Jennings has a teacher aide in the classroom to help monitor students' work at the different rotations, and to get students started with the iPad practice exercises.

All students have a chance to rotate through each of the activities, giving each a chance to demonstrate their understanding in a variety of ways. Ms. Jennings is able to assess students' understanding through the small group work, workbook pages, and data provided by Khan Academy.

Reflection Questions

Now that you've read about Ms. Jennings's lesson, consider her technology use. She selected technologies to engage and assess her students.

- Would you consider this a technology-rich lesson? Why or why not?

- What was the specific purpose of Ms. Jennings's technology use in this lesson?

- How did Ms. Jennings's integration of technology advance the teaching and learning of math in this lesson?

- What were she and/or the students able to do with technology that was different from or better than what could have been done without technology?

- How did Ms. Jennings use technology as an assessment tool?

Now, consider the math teaching practices in her lesson.

- What were Ms. Jennings's goals for this math lesson?

- To what extent did students have equitable access to learn and demonstrate their understanding in this lesson?

- Overall, what strengths do you see in this lesson? What opportunities do you notice?

- How did Ms. Jennings elicit and build upon students' mathematical thinking?

● ● ● ●

What Does the Research Say?

The following research supports the use of technology as an assessment tool:

- The U.S. Department of Education's Office of Educational Technology suggests that the transition from pencil–paper to digital assessments will enable a number of shifts. The shifts that technology makes possible include embedding assessment within, instead of after, learning;

incorporating universal design principles for increased accessibility; enabling adaptive rather than fixed assessment pathways; providing real-time machine feedback rather than delayed teacher feedback; and allowing multimedia assessment items rather than generic multiple choice.

- Technology provides assessment data that was previously inaccessible to educators, parents, and students. In fact, technology has given rise to entirely new fields such as learning analytics and data mining. Many programs now offer teachers (and parents or students) dashboards of data summarizing potentially relevant assessment information in a single snap-shot. However, leveraging voluminous amounts of data requires expanded data literacy on the part of teachers. "Big data" has also given rise to new ethical concerns about privacy. Nevertheless, studies indicate that making assessment data more accessible to teachers can lead to better differenti-ation for students' individual needs and more responsive teaching. Using technology as an assessment tool offers affordances and emerging chal-lenges for educators, and new questions for researchers.

- Assessment is an ongoing focus in K–12 education, and technology plays an increasing role. The use of technology as a high-stakes assessment tool makes voluminous amounts of data available for analysis and data-driven decision making. This has coincided with high-stakes assessment policy requirements since the 2001 No Child Left Behind Act. Many schools and states are transitioning to computer-based high-stakes assessments in math.

- Computer-based testing affords greater efficiency for schools and stake-holders. On the other hand, it can exacerbate inequities that already exist with regard to high-stakes testing. In order to implement computer-based testing, schools must have access to hardware, software, and digital infra-structure for all students. Computer-based tests must also attend to the needs of bilingual learners and special education populations.

The following research addresses leveraging students' mathematical understanding:

- Although high-stakes, summative assessment has driven policy in math education, much research has focused on formative classroom assessment. The National Mathematics Advisory Panel (2008) found that, "…teachers' regular use of formative assessment improves their students' learning" (p. xxiii). A positive association between formative assessment and improved student learning outcomes has been documented in multiple studies (e.g., Black & Wiliam, 1998a, 1998b; Hattie, 2009; Popham, 2008). Whereas summative assessments measure students' learning of math, formative assessments focus on data and feedback for learning. By eliciting what students know and can do during a lesson, teachers can make instructional decisions to adapt and better address students' learning needs (Leahy, Lyon, Thompson, & William, 2005; Wiliam, 2011).

- Eliciting and interpreting students' mathematical thinking enables teachers to appropriately respond and build upon student ideas. Multiple studies in math education focus on professional noticing of children's mathematical thinking which includes: "a) attending to children's strategies, (b) interpreting children's understandings, and (c) deciding how to respond on the basis of children's understandings" (Jacobs, Lamb, & Philipp, 2010, p. 169). What teachers notice and attend to can have a significant impact on students' learning experiences.

- Assessing math learning means more than determining if answers are right or wrong. Recognizing misconceptions, error patterns, and difficulties enables teachers to diagnose and address incorrect or incomplete ideas early, before students practice and internalize them (e.g., NCTM, 2014; Schifter, 2001; Swan, 2001). To do so, teachers can design questions and tasks that purposefully elicit common errors and misconceptions (e.g., Bray, 2013; Swan, 2001). Incorporating a variety of assessment strategies also gives students an opportunity to demonstrate what and how they know, not just whether their answer is correct or not. Integrating formative assessment that notices and attends to student reasoning, including misconceptions, is a crucial component of effective math teaching practices.

Reflecting on Technology in Math Teaching

As you read the cases of Mr. Evers's and Ms. Jennings's kindergarten classrooms, you may have noticed several similarities and differences. Some of the big ideas are summarized in Table 4.1.

A possible perspective for comparing Mr. Evers and Ms. Jennings's technology use in these lessons might be to ask, *"How is technology used to assess students' mathematical understanding?"* Both teachers used technology in multiple ways throughout the lesson. Although Mr. Evers leverages shared student devices for individual online assessments at the end of the lesson, Ms. Jennings incorporates formative assessment in interactive slides as well as individual online assessment on devices at the end of the lesson. She designed tasks to elicit students' misconceptions about shapes and orientation, addressed those misconceptions through an activity that involved manipulative shapes, and continued to assess students' understanding of shapes in a variety of ways at the end of the lesson. Mr. Evers used assessment as a way to gauge what students had learned, whereas Ms. Jennings used assessment as a way to guide and inform her teaching and, in turn, what students were learning successfully.

TABLE 4.1 Use of Technology in the Cases of Mr. Evers and Ms. Jennings

	The Case of Mr. Evers	The Case of Ms. Jennings
What technology is used?	Teacher iPad and projector, shared student computers, virtual manipulative, IXL practice exercises online	Teacher computer and projector, shared student iPads, virtual manipulative, Khan Academy practice exercises online
What math is emphasized?	Identifying various types of 2D shapes.	Identifying various types of 2D shapes.
How is the lesson launched?	Mr. Evers shows a sing-and-dance-along video about shapes to begin the lesson.	Ms. Jennings displays a slide with four shapes and the class discusses the shape names.
Who is doing the math in this lesson?	Students identify shapes and work in a whole-group setting to create shapes using virtual pattern blocks. Students work individually on shape identification activities and an online assessment.	Students work in groups to identify shapes. They individually create shape drawings with physical pattern blocks and discuss the shape names in small groups. Students also work individually on shape identification activities and an online assessment.
When and how is technology used in the lesson?	The beginning of the lesson is conveyed with a projected teacher device. The end of the lesson includes computers as one of three rotations.	The beginning of the lesson is conveyed through interactive slides using a teacher device and shared student iPads. The end of the lesson includes iPads used for individual assessment in one of four rotations.

We can also examine how technology contributed to equitable math learning experiences for all children in each class. Both lessons enabled students to participate in math discussion with the whole group and in small groups. Furthermore, all students in both classes had an opportunity to interact with technology. Ms. Jennings's lesson included audio options for early readers and physical manipulatives that would be more accessible to students with vision impairments. Ms. Jennings's varied forms of assessment at the end of the lesson enabled each student to demonstrate their understanding in multiple ways.

Recommendations for Practice

This chapter began with the question: *Instead of using technology as a tool for assessment of mathematical learning, what if we leverage technology as a tool to assess for learning?* Classroom cases of Mr. Evers and Ms. Jennings address this question. Whereas Mr. Evers uses technology-based assessment to find out what students do or don't know, Ms. Jennings leverages technology for formative assessment to reveal misconceptions and to inform her teaching during the lesson. Here are three practical suggestions for using technology as both a formative and summative assessment tool in your classroom.

1. Use technology to elicit what students know and understand during a lesson.

Interactive features through tools such as Pear Deck and Desmos allow teachers to pose strategic questions and gauge student understanding within lessons. Other tools include clicker devices (or apps) and the Plickers app through which a single teacher device can quickly summarize responses from cards that students display. Both options allow teachers to pose multiple-choice questions and quickly display summaries of students' responses. Such options are anonymous, and can be used to highlight common misconceptions in a way that might be more comfortable for students and teachers who are just beginning to leverage errors as part of learning.

2. Use technology to document not only students' products, but also their processes.

Ms. Jennings used photos to capture students' pattern block creations and recreated them using a virtual manipulative. (She could also have just displayed the photo images.) You can capture students' authentic work and display it for class discussion using technologies common in many classrooms, (e.g., document camera, cell phone/tablet/camera, scanner, and screenshots). Using technology to document student work opens new possibilities for how students could show their work, potentially incorporating physical or virtual manipulatives, drawings, or visual models. In this way, teachers can rely on a broader array of evidence when assessing student work.

In addition to tools that capture the results of student work, technology also offers exciting opportunities to capture strategies and processes. Screencasting tools allow students to record their voice and writing as they solve problems. Video and audio tools can be used in a similar fashion. In a classroom with many students and only one teacher, technology tools can provide a window into students' mathematical thought processes that might otherwise be accessible only through one-on-one interactions.

3. Use data conveyed in teacher dashboards to inform your instruction.

Many popular platforms such as IXL, Khan Academy, and curriculum-based digital resources provide voluminous amounts of student assessment data on teacher dashboards. Take a closer look at what this data tells you about student understanding. Besides how many exercises students get right or wrong, are multiple students Ms.ing the same question or giving the same incorrect answer? If so, this could indicate a shared misconception. Are some students getting perfect scores but only by taking many attempts? This could be a sign that students are using immediate feedback to guess until they get problems correct, regardless of their actual understanding. Are some students correctly finishing all of their exercises in no time? Consider more appropriately challenging material. Learning to effectively use teacher dashboard data to inform your teaching is a way that technology can support assessment for learning.

Connecting Cases with Standards

In this chapter, the cases of Mr. Evers and Ms. Jennings illustrate two approaches to technology-enabled assessment during a lesson on identifying shapes. The standards identified below indicate alignment with Common Core State Standards for Mathematics, and ISTE Standards for Students and for Educators. You might also consider alignment with math standards in your state or district, as well as ISTE Standards for Administrators and for Coaches.

Math Content Standards

CCSS.MATH.CONTENT.K.G.A.2. Correctly name shapes regardless of their orientations or overall size.

CCSS.MATH.CONTENT.K.G.B.4. Analyze and compare two- and three-dimensional shapes in different sizes and orientations, using informal language to describe their similarities, differences, parts (e.g., number of sides and vertices/"corners") and other attributes (e.g., having sides of equal length).

Mathematical Practice Standards

- Use appropriate tools strategically

- Attend to precision

- Look for and make use of structure

ISTE Standards for Educators

5a.   Use technologies to create, adapt and personalize learning experiences that foster independent learning and accommodate learner differences and needs.

5b.   Design authentic learning activities that align with content area standards and use digital tools and resources to maximize learning.

5c.   Explore and apply instructional design principles to create innovative digital learning environments that engage and support active, deep learning.

6a.   Foster a culture where students take ownership of their learning goals and outcomes in both independent and group settings.

6b.   Manage the use of technology and student learning strategies in digital platforms, virtual environments, hands-on makerspaces or in the field.

6d.   Model and nurture creativity and creative expression to communicate ideas, knowledge or connections.

7a.   Provide alternative ways for students to demonstrate competency and reflect on their learning using technology.

7b.   Use technology to design and implement a variety of formative and summative assessments that accommodate learner needs, provide timely feedback to students and inform instruction.

7c.   Use assessment data to guide progress and communicate with students, parents and education stakeholders to build student self-direction.

ISTE Standards for Students

1c.   Students use technology to seek feedback that informs and improves their practice and to demonstrate their learning in a variety of ways.

6c.   Students communicate complex ideas clearly and effectively by creating or using a variety of digital objects such as visualizations, models or simulations.

MOVING FROM TEACHER-CENTERED TO STUDENT-CENTERED INSTRUCTION

● Instead of teacher-centered instruction in math, what if we
● used technology as a representational tool to support more
● student-centered learning experiences?

IN THIS CHAPTER, you will find two cases that take place in fifth-grade classrooms where they are learning about line plots. Teachers in both cases utilize technology as part of their lessons, but you will notice some big differences between the two. After you read each case, consider how the lesson aligns with math content and process standards, and technology standards for students and/or educators. Compare your ideas with the alignment at the end of the chapter. After each case, take time to reflect and, if you have the opportunity, discuss with others. Once you've had a chance to read and think carefully about the similarities and differences between the two cases, the chapter includes a summary of what research has to say about: *Technology as a Representational Tool* and *Empowering Student-Driven Mathematics.* Consider how the cases and research connect with your own practice, as well as the recommendations for practice toward the end of the chapter.

Technology as a Representational Tool

Teachers frequently use technology to plan and deliver math lessons. Slides and presentation tools (e.g., PowerPoint, Prezi, and Google Slides) are commonly used in college and K–12 classrooms, and some textbook publishers include slides with their math curriculum. Slides can be useful ways to organize and convey information, but traditional slides are demonstrative in nature, and display only static representations. Digital technologies allow us to go beyond demonstration, enabling interactivity among students and teachers and dynamic mathematical representations. Rather than a teacher using technology to show or tell students about a mathematical idea, interactive tools allow students to be more participatory in the learning experience, and to connect among dynamic mathematical representations.

Empowering Student-Driven Math Learning

Math can empower students to investigate, understand, and even change the world around them. Knowing and understanding math is essential for school, college, and career. Math can also be a useful tool for analyzing issues that are important in students' lives and in society at large. Student-centered math teaching supports the development of positive mathematical identities by positioning all students as capable mathematicians. Furthermore, teaching that leverages authentic contexts, including problems that relate to students' lives, empower not only important math, but also other subject areas and broader societal issues.

Ms. Dylan's Grade 5 class is learning to create and use line plots for measuring data in fractions of a unit. She knows that technology enables a lot of access to real-world data and wants to use that information in this lesson. As you read this case, consider how technology is used for teaching and learning and ways in which this lesson is teacher- or student-centered.

 **CASE 5.1**

Ms. Dylan's Grade 5 Class: Line Plots and Measurement Data

OBJECTIVES

- Create line plots for data measured in fractional units.
- Solve problems using data in line plots.

Ms. Dylan is teaching a lesson about creating and using line plots for data that is measured in fractions. Students should have learned about line plots in fourth grade, but she wants to review in case some students do not understand or remember. Her goals are for students to access a data set online to make a line plot and then answer questions about it. She wants to use real-world data, and because there has been some extreme weather in her area recently, she decides to use annual precipitation data she finds online. The data is measured in decimals, but because her class learned about fractions, decimals, and rounding earlier this year, she decides they should be able to round the decimal amounts to the nearest fourth of an inch.

Fifth graders in Ms. Dylan's school switch classes for math, and she has the so-called "middle" group of students who tend to score "proficient" on their state math assessments. As her math group enters the classroom, she displays a warm-up word problem on the whiteboard (today's is a logic puzzle about buckets of water) for students to solve as she collects homework from the night before. Once this routine is complete, she begins the day's lesson by displaying and saying the lesson objectives, and asks students if they remember what line plots look like. Most students nod affirmatively, so Ms. Dylan proceeds with subsequent slides that show how line plots are set up and labelled.

Ms. Dylan makes sure to read the slides aloud, sometimes inviting students to read them, and she always adds some additional explanation to help students understand what she wants them to know. As she explains each part of the line plot (units, labels, title, Xs to plot data points) she demonstrates how to create a line plot using a table of rainfall totals she found online (with the line projected on the whiteboard, she is able to draw Xs for data points). Because the data is shown in decimals, and the line graph is labelled in fractional inches, she says they will round rainfall measurements to the nearest fourth inch. She frequently calls on students who raise their hands to say the corresponding fraction for each decimal amount. Some students struggle to round numbers like 2.7 to the nearest fourth inch. Instead of rounding to 2 3/4, they round up to three. She reminds the class that one-quarter = 0.25, and three-quarters = 0.75.

After using the slides to explain and demonstrate how to create a line plot, Ms. Dylan wants the class to make one together. This time she hands out a worksheet with data about local annual snowfall from the last nine years and projects the Number Line app from Math Learning Center (apps.mathlearningcenter.org/number-line) on the board, which displays a basic number line with whole numbers. She adjusts the labels to the nearest fourth inch and scrolls until the numbers show the range that fits the data.

She asks students to recreate the line plot on their worksheets as the class works together. Students take turns coming to the board and drawing Xs to represent the snowfall data Ms. Dylan has provided. At the end of this activity, it appears that most students are catching on, so she decides to ask questions about the line plot they created together (the same questions are on their worksheet). The questions include: What is the difference between the greatest snowfall amount and the least snowfall amount? How many years has snowfall been above 20 inches? What is the total snowfall over the last nine years? Ms. Dylan gives students time to work, and calls on volunteers to explain how they found their answers. She expects the last question to be challenging for many students, so she calls on a student who is usually successful.

After the whole-group instruction, Ms. Dylan asks students to flip over their worksheet and work on the back side individually. The worksheet includes a chart to fill in the average annual precipitation for twelve cities chosen by the student. She tells students they can use one of their own devices, or one of the classroom tablets to look up the information they need. She prepared QR codes to several websites with historical weather data. Students are required to find data for each city and list the rainfall in inches in decimal form (shown on the websites), round to the nearest fourth inch, and create a line plot to display their data. She is pleased that the activity requires students to use internet resources to find authentic data. The questions on the worksheet are similar to those she asked during the whole-class activity: What is the difference between the greatest precipitation amount and the least precipitation amount? How many cities had annual precipitation above 40 inches? What is the total precipitation for all of the cities you selected?

She knows that not all students have access to a computer at home to look up the information they need, so she encourages them to complete their data table during class time and finish the questions outside of class as homework.

Reflection Questions

Consider how Ms. Dylan used technology in this lesson. She used technology to display content on slides, to project a line and create a graph, and for students to access authentic data online.

- Would you consider this a technology-rich lesson? Why or why not?

- How did Ms. Dylan's integration of technology advance the teaching and learning of math in this lesson?

- To what extent did technology empower students as math learners?

- How did Ms. Dylan use technology as a representational tool?

Now, consider the math teaching practices in Ms. Dylan's lesson.

- What were Ms. Dylan's goals for this math lesson?

- To what extent did students have equitable access to learn and demonstrate their understanding in this lesson?

- Overall, what strengths do you see in this lesson? What opportunities do you notice?

- Would you categorize this lesson as more teacher-centered or more student-centered? Why?

- What math challenges and errors would you anticipate students might experience in this lesson?

● ● ● ●

Mr. Harriet's Grade 5 class is also learning about line plots. The next case describes how he integrates technology into his lesson and math teaching practices. Consider how he uses technology as a representational tool. Is the lesson more teacher-centered or student-centered?

 ## CASE 5.2

Mr. Harriet's Grade 5 Lesson: Line Plots and Measurement Data

OBJECTIVES
- Create line plots for data measured in fractional units.
- Solve problems using data in line plots.

Mr. Harriet teaches in a rural agricultural area. His class is learning about fractions, measurement, and data. They have also been learning about water conservation in science. For today's lesson, Mr. Harriet decided to expand the procedural treatment of line plots in his math textbook, and will instead integrate these two ideas along with a connection to their local community, which recently experienced flooding. In this way, the class can use math as a tool to help students understand science and the world around them. Several students in the class have smartphones or tablets and he has some classroom tablets as well. They'll use their devices in today's lesson.

For the past few weeks, students have been focused on water in science: water conservation, the distribution of saltwater and freshwater on Earth, and the role of water in plant growth.

Mr. Harriet's students have been working in pairs to grow bean plants under three different conditions: each group has one plant that they barely water, one plant that they overwater, and one plant that they water appropriately. All other conditions (e.g., sunlight, soil quantity and quality, and temperature) have been held constant to the greatest extent possible. When they began the project, he had students place rulers in the cups where they are growing the plants, each placed perpendicular to ground, with the ruler touching the bottom of the cup. They also labelled each plant at the top of the cup, with *Too Much, Not Enough,* or *Correct Amount.* The day before this lesson, Mr. Harriet had students use their smartphones or tablets to take photos of the plants to show their height, as measured on the rulers in the cups.

To begin the lesson, Mr. Harriet displays the interactive Number Line app from Math Learning Center on the board (apps.mathlearningcenter.org/number-line), displaying a number line that starts at zero, and is labelled by units of one, as shown in Figure 5.1.

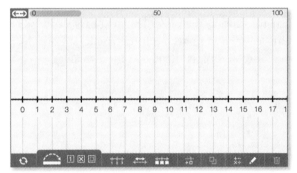

Figure 5.1 Interactive number line.

He also hands out rulers that measure to the nearest one-eighth inch and small sticky notes. He asks students to measure the length of their pinky fingers to the nearest one-eighth inch, and write the length on the sticky note. He encourages them to work with a neighbor. While students are working, he circulates to observe how they are measuring and what complications they are encountering. After a few minutes, he notices major inconsistencies where students are beginning and ending their measurements, and addresses this with the class: "I notice that many of you are starting your pinky measurement at different points, and there is some confusion about whether or not to include fingernails. Why do things like this matter when we're taking measurements?"

Several students raise their hands and Mr. Harriet calls on Angelica. "We all have to measure the same way so that they mean the same thing." He agrees, adding that the measurements need to be taken in similar ways so that they can compare the data. He asks students for suggestions on where to start their measurements, and they collectively decide to measure with their palms facing up and position the ruler at the point where their pinky finger begins, next to the ring finger. By popular vote, the students decide not to include the length of fingernails. The class remeasures and writes their updated measurements on sticky notes. As students finish their measurements, he asks them to place their sticky note above the correct location on the number line displayed on the board. The class attempts to do so, resulting in a line plot with the data all clustered around the two and three.

Referring to the line plot, Mr. Harriet asks whether the graph represents the data in a useful way. The class agrees it does not. He asks what they could do to make it more useful. Several students suggest changing the labels to one-eighth inch, because that is the unit they used to make their measurements. (This is what Mr. Harriet had hoped students would realize!) He shows them how to quickly change the representation within the interactive number line app. He adjusts the labels on the number line, scrolls so that the screen displays a range that includes two and three, and then asks students to each move one sticky note to its new correct location (as shown in Figure 5.2).

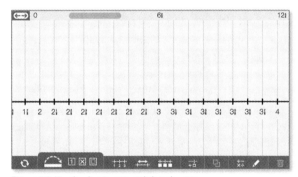

Figure 5.2 Number line in one-eighth inch units.

The result is a line plot that represents each student's pinky finger length. He writes a title below the number line, "Pinky Lengths of Students in Mr. Harriet's Class," and reminds students that data representations should always include descriptive labels. Mr. Harriet poses questions to students about the data, such as "What is the most typical length of pinky fingers in this class?" and "What is the range between the longest pinky finger and the shortest?"

At the end of the opening activity, Mr. Harriet explains that they are going to use line plots to represent and better understand data from the bean plants they have been growing. He displays a QR code that leads students to a file with all of their plant photos from the day before. He asks students to work in groups of three and gives each group three copies of a number line with tick marks, but no labels. Students are to create line plots that show the heights, to the nearest one-eighth inch, of plants that received too much water, not enough water, and the correct amount of water.

Students engage in conversations about the measurements of the plant shown in each photo, sometimes disagreeing initially and then discussing until they reach a consensus. Some students record the measurements in a list. A few students ask if they can use an app on their phone to automatically measure the plant heights right now and Mr. Harriet encourages them to give it a try! One group makes three tables, one for each plant condition, with a column for the plant number and a column for the measurement. A couple groups do not write down their measurements, instead directly record their results as Xs on the line plots. One of these groups immediately labels the number lines starting at zero. They find that the scale was insufficient for recording their data, and have to start over. The other group records their first measurement in the middle of the graph, which seems to work out for two of the three conditions, but they end up having to get another blank copy of the number line to create a different scale for the third condition (Correct amount of water).

When the class is done making their line plots, Mr. Harriet asks students to compare their plots with other groups to see how they are similar and different. Students notice that the data in the plots tend to have similar overall shape, but individual measures are not exactly the same. This invites another quick conversation about measurement error, and then Mr. Harriet asks the class what they notice about the three different line plots. The class observes that the plants with the correct amount of water have the most variation and the tallest heights. They also notice that the over-watered plants have the least variation and low heights. Although the under-watered plants also have low heights, the data was more spread out. From these observations, Mr. Harriet asks students to find the range for each of their line plots to verify their observations (and to apply subtracting fractions in context, in accordance with the grade-level math standards).

To conclude the lesson, Mr. Harriet asks students what they think their data might suggest about farm crops for the upcoming year. Students quickly make the connection that recent floods may result in less plant growth in agriculture, too. To extend this exploration, Mr. Harriet directs students to the website **water.weather.gov/precip** where they can use an interactive map to look up their town and find its amount of precipitation for the last 10 years. He asks students how they might represent the data about annual precipitation, and whether a line plot would be the best choice for the data. Over the next couple of days, students will use online data sources to locate data about annual rainfall and crop yield in their area, make predictions, and draw conclusions from their data. They'll meet virtually with a water scientist and an agronomist from a regional university to learn more about relationships among water, crops, and the environment.

Mr. Harriet is pleased that not only did students represent data on line plots and use interactive tools to access and represent data, they also strengthened their understanding of water science and related it to recent climate events in their local community.

Reflection Questions

Consider how Mr. Harriet used technology in this lesson.

- Would you consider this a technology-rich lesson? Why or why not?

- What was the specific purpose of Mr. Harriet's technology use in this lesson?

- To what extent did technology empower students as mathematical learners?

- How did Mr. Harriet use technology a representational tool?

Consider the math teaching practices in Mr. Harriet's lesson.

- What were Mr. Harriet's math instructional goals for this lesson? Were they achieved?

- To what extent did students have equitable access to learn and demonstrate their understanding in this lesson?

- Overall, what strengths do you see in this lesson? What opportunities do you notice?

- Would you categorize this lesson as more teacher-centered or more student-centered? Why?

- What math challenges and errors would you anticipate students might experience in this lesson?

● ● ● ●

What Does the Research Say?

The following research findings support the use of technology as a representational tool:

- NCTM identifies *Use and Connect mathematical representations* as one of eight effective mathematics teaching practices. When students make connections among contextual, visual, verbal, physical, and symbolic representations (Lesh, Post, & Behr, 1987), the variety of perspectives help them deepen their understanding of mathematical concepts (Tripathi, 2008).

Visual representations, in particular, can be powerful ways to expand access to emergent bilinguals and struggling learners (Fuson & Murata, 2007). Connecting among dynamic digital representations and mathematical models supports students with visualizing mathematical relationships and concepts (Roschelle et al, 2010).

- Technology-enabled dynamic representations allow users to manipulate math objects, quickly explore numerous iterations or math scenarios, and visualize how connected representations change and are connected. Dynamic geometry environments (DGEs) support geometric constructions that can be quickly changed by dragging points in infinitely many locations. Computer algebra systems permit students to make and test conjectures while saving tedious, time-consuming computation and algebraic manipulation. Overall, the types of dynamic representations afforded by technology tools impact how students can visualize and interact with math, and open up new opportunities for deep mathematical discussion about explorations that would be impractical or impossible with pencil and paper alone.

- When evaluating technology for use in math lessons, teachers in one study tended to associate dynamic, interactive representations with transformative technology integration, whereas static, fixed representations corresponded with integrating technology as a mere replacement (Hughes, Thomas, & Scharber, 2006; Thomas & Edson, 2017). Teachers in the study also associated transformative technology integration with not only showing representations, but also connecting and discussing among multiple, often dynamic, representations.

The following research addresses empowering student-driven math learning:

- The guidelines for assessment and instruction in statistics education (GAISE) (Franklin et al., 2005), offer a framework of three levels through which students progress. It is appropriate for beginning students to use data from a classroom census or simple experiment, and begin to compare data from one group to another. As students transition to the second level, they begin to use data distributions as tools for analysis and acknowledge that looking beyond specific data can tell a larger story. The fifth-grade students in Mr. Harriet's class incorporate aspects of Level A and, through their exploration and connection with broader context in science and agriculture, begin to engage in Level B statistical thinking. Not only are learning progressions important for statistical understanding, understanding levels of geometric thought (Burger & Shaughnessy, 1986; van Hiele, 1980), and learning trajectories about number and operations (Clements & Sarama, 2009), also help teachers design learning experiences that are developmentally appropriate and better meet students' needs.

- Research and discussion about teacher- and student-centered teaching date back more than a century to the reform era of John Dewey. The constructivist learning theories of Piaget and sociocultural theories of Vygotsky emphasize student-centered learning. Active construction of knowledge and building mathematical understanding through discourse centers students in the learning experience, whereas traditional, teacher-centered approaches position students as passive recipients of disciplinary knowledge. Student-centered instruction enables teachers to respond to students' needs and develop positive identities as math learners.

- Math teaching that promotes equitable access for all students affirms and builds upon students' identities and contexts. "Effective teachers draw on community resources to understand how they can use contexts, culture, conditions, and language to support mathematics teaching and learning" (NCTM, 2014, p. 65; Berry & Ellis, 2013; Cross et al., 2012; Kisker et al., 2012; Moschkovich, 1999, 2011; Planas & Civil, 2013). Drawing upon culture and relevant contexts is one aspect of teaching math for social justice, an approach that can deepen students' understanding of social issues, motivate mathematical learning, and highlight math as a tool to understand the world (Gutstein & Peterson, 2013; Larson, 2017). When teachers provide equitable opportunities to use technology to solve rich math problems about important contexts, all students benefit.

Reflecting on Technology in Math Teaching

As you read the cases of Ms. Dylan's and Mr. Harriet's Grade 5 classrooms, you probably compared their teaching to one another, and perhaps to your own classroom or those you have observed. Table 5.1 offers a comparative summary of some aspects of the two cases.

TABLE 5.1 Use of Technology in the Cases of Ms. Dylan and Mr. Harriet

	The Case of Ms. Dylan	The Case of Mr. Harriet
What technology is used?	Slides and projector, interactive number line, QR codes, online data sources	Teacher device and projector, interactive number line, cameras on student devices, QR codes linked to photo files, interactive online maps and data sources
What math is emphasized?	Creating and solving problems about line plots with data measured in fractional units.	Creating and solving problems about line plots with data measured in fractional units.
How is the lesson launched?	Ms. Dylan gives a warm-up problem, states the objective, and asks students what they remember about the topic.	Mr. Harriet immediately engages students in collecting and representing measurement data about the length of their pinky fingers.
Who is doing the math in this lesson?	Ms. Dylan shows students how to create line plots from online data, creates a line plot with student input, and then asks students to make their own plots.	Students collect measurement data from their fingers and photos of the plants they grew. Students create line plots as a whole group and in small groups.
When and how is technology used in the lesson?	Slides are used to convey instruction about how to make a line plot. The class uses an interactive number line as a background to create a line plot. Students access online data through digital devices.	The class uses an interactive number line and adjusts its parameters to create a line plot on the board. Students use personal devices and QR codes to access photos of their plants, some students use an interactive app to measure their plants. The class uses interactive map data and online data.

Although the two teachers in these cases use similar technologies for teaching, one might wonder: *"How does technology help students create and understand line plots in these two lessons?"* Ms. Dylan uses slides to show and tell students how to create line plots, projects a number line app for the class to create a line plot, and requires students to access online data for their homework assignment. Mr. Harriet, on the other hand, uses the same number line in a way that shows the need for precision on a line plot and highlights the dynamic nature of the app for adjusting measurement scales. Students use their own devices to access data they had collected as part of a science experiment, and draw upon other online, interactive resources to connect their line plots with science, agriculture, and their local environment. In addition, Mr. Harriet uses technology to virtually connect students with experts in the fields of water science and agronomy.

Technology supported the two teachers' math teaching practices, particularly with respect to student-centeredness. Ms. Dylan used a more teacher-centered approach to teaching, using technology to show students procedures for creating line plots and identifying the specific sites where they could locate the data she wanted them to plot. Ms. Dylan did use local data to try to interest students, but they did not have an opportunity to measure or collect authentic data or to interpret in the context of their own lives and experiences. Furthermore, by selecting data that was represented in decimal form, students may have focused as much on rounding to the nearest quarter-inch, as they did the math objectives for the lesson. Some of the comparison questions Ms. Dylan asked students made little sense in context. For instance, why would anyone need to know the total amount of precipitation for all of the cities students selected? One might say that she selected a context to serve the math, but the math did not always make sense in the context.

Mr. Harriet employed a more student-centered approach, beginning with a chance for students to collect authentic measurement data and then discover an appropriate scale for a line plot. Throughout this lesson, students collected authentic data and related their observations to themselves, what they were learning in science, and their local community. Mr. Harriet's students were able to not only create line plots, but also see how line plots could help make sense of data that mattered in the real world around them. After the lesson, students engaged in an extended task where they compared predictions and data from their own experiments, and line plots with annual data about precipitation and crop yields and then talk to experts to deepen their understanding about the context. In Mr. Harriet's lesson, math served the context, enabling students to predict and understand the results of their experiment, the results that contributed to further science learning.

Recommendations for Practice

We began this chapter by asking: *Instead of teacher-centered instruction in math, what if we use technology as an interactive tool to support more student-centered learning experiences?* Cases from Ms. Dylan's and Mr. Harriet's classrooms offer a sense of how that shift might look in a lesson about data. In your own classroom, consider the following recommendations for leveraging technology as an interactive tool that supports student-centered instruction.

1. Use interactive features to engage students in mathematical exploration.

If a picture is worth a thousand words, what might be the value of an interactive tool with countless visualizations? Ms. Dylan's and Mr. Harriet used an interactive number line in their lessons. Many virtual manipulatives offer interactive features. Base ten block apps often allow you to instantaneously group and ungroup blocks, immediately illustrating place value relationships. With dynamic geometry environments (DGEs) such as Geogebra, Cabri, or Geometer's Sketchpad, children can drag shapes to show infinite versions. Sliders within DGEs allow students to visualize the impact of various parameters on graphs or shapes. For instance, what happens to the sides of a triangle when one of the angles increases or decreases? Or how does the graph of a line change when the slope goes from positive to negative? Dynamic, interactive technologies enable visualizations and potential connections across mathematical representations that are not otherwise possible with fixed images.

2. Use technology to connect students with people and contexts that are relevant to their lives.

Word problems and applications are often intended to show math in the "real world," but are those problems real and relevant for students, or are they fake and contrived? Few students will find intrinsic value in knowing the volume of a hypothetical rectangular swimming pool with a constant depth of five feet. But they might care about the volume of a raised garden bed they need to fill with soil for a school garden. Or, they could use online design tools to design a raised garden bed and explore the cost of soil from local garden supply stores—making the math real for students' lives. Technology can also be employed for students to access and understand math in relation to broader social issues. Mr. Harriet's lesson might explore more deeply issues of climate change and how it impacts agriculture in their rural area. Instead of solving worksheets involving or in contrived contexts students could apply proportional reasoning using online electoral data to investigate gerrymandering of legislative districts in their state to consider issues of representation. In this respect, student-centered teaching with technology not only empowers students to build their understanding of math, but also discover how math can be used as a tool for understanding their world and lived experiences.

Connecting Cases with Standards

The cases of Ms. Dylan and Mr. Harriet highlight technology as a representational tool and student-centered approaches to teaching. The standards identified below indicate alignment with Common Core State Standards for Mathematics, and ISTE Standards for Students and for Educators. You might also consider alignment with math standards in your state or district, as well as ISTE Standards for Administrators and for Coaches.

Math Content Standard

CCSS.MATH.CONTENT.5.MD.B.2. Make a line plot to display a data set of measurements in fractions of a unit (1/2, 1/4, 1/8). Use operations on fractions for this grade to solve problems involving information presented in line plots.

Mathematical Practice Standards

- Construct viable arguments and critique the reasoning of others.
- Model with mathematics.
- Use appropriate tools strategically.
- Attend to precision.

ISTE Standards for Educators

3b.   Establish a learning culture that promotes curiosity and critical examination of online resources and fosters digital literacy and media fluency.

4c.   Use collaborative tools to expand students' authentic, real-world learning experiences by engaging virtually with experts, teams and students, locally and globally.

5b.   Design authentic learning activities that align with content area standards and use digital tools and resources to maximize active, deep learning.

5c.   Explore and apply instructional design principles to create innovative digital learning environments that engage and support learning.

6a.   Foster a culture where students take ownership of their learning goals and outcomes in both independent and group settings.

ISTE Standards for Students

3d.   Students build knowledge by actively exploring real-world issues and problems, developing ideas and theories and pursing answers and solutions.

5b.   Students collect data or identify relevant data sets, use digital tools to analyze them, and represent data in various ways to facilitate problem-solving and decision-making.

6c.   Students communicate complex ideas clearly and effectively by creating or using a variety of digital objects such as visualizations, models or simulations.

7b.   Students use collaborative technologies to work with others, including peers, experts or community members, to examine issues and problems from multiple viewpoints.

MOVING FROM TECHNOLOGY FOR ITS OWN SAKE TO TECHNOLOGY FOR RICH MATH LEARNING

● Instead of using technology for its own sake, what if
● we used technology in the service of learning rich,
● interesting math?

IN THIS CHAPTER, you will get a glimpse of two grade-four classrooms where technology is used as part of a lesson about angles and polygons. While you're reading, think about the extent to which technology is supporting math learning in these two cases. You may also examine how each of the lessons aligns with standards for math content and practices, ISTE Standards for students and educators, and comparing what you find with the alignment at the end of this chapter. After reading and reflecting upon the two cases, compare your insights and connections with what research has to say about two big ideas illustrated in the cases: *Technology as an Educational Tool and Teaching and Learning Mathematics with Technology.*

Technology as an Educational Tool

Technology is important and worth learning about in its own right. Digital tools continue to enable innovations in school, society, and the workplace. Automation, artificial intelligence, virtual reality, and new avenues for communication and connectivity will continue to transform the world in which students live and will one day work. It is important for students to learn about innovative technologies, and to gain the technological literacy required for life in the digital age. But when, in a crowded school curriculum, can students have the opportunities needed to develop technological literacy? Although math thinking and learning are inextricably linked with cutting edge technologies, students and teachers do not always recognize connections between math learning and technology. Through carefully-designed instructional activities, students can develop technological skills in the context of learning math. Such an approach positions even the most cutting-edge digital tools, not as toys, but as educational tools. Using innovative technologies as educational tools aligned with standards for math learning also opens up more time and opportunities for students to develop technological literacy during regular class time.

Teaching and Learning Math with Technology

The NCTM Tool and Technology Principle reads: "An excellent mathematics program integrates the use of mathematical tools and technology as essential resources to help students learn and make sense of mathematical ideas, reason mathematically, and communicate their mathematical thinking" (2014, p. 78). It is not enough to integrate technology into a math class if that technology is not helping students learn, make sense, reason, and communicate about math. At the same time, technology is widely used to do math in the real world, and it is imperative that students learn with, and are prepared for using, tools of the trade. Through strategic use of technology, students can develop deeper understanding of geometry, measurement, algebra, numbers, and data.

Ms. Baker is teaching her fourth-grade class a lesson about drawing and recognizing angles and lines. To what extent is technology used as an educational tool during her lesson? In what ways are students learning math through the use of technology?

 CASE 6.1

Ms. Baker's Grade 4 Lesson on Drawing and Identifying Lines and Angles

OBJECTIVES
- Draw lines, line segments, rays, and angles
- Identify angles and lines in polygons
- Explore new coding robots

Ms. Baker's students recently began a geometry unit. Today, they'll be learning to draw lines, line segments, rays, and angles. They'll also work on identifying types of angles and lines in polygons.

Recently, Ms. Baker went to a conference where she learned about some coding robots and heard about how other teachers were using robots to get their kids excited about learning. She was so impressed that she applied for classroom funding to purchase a few coding robots for her own classroom. Today is the first day she'll be using the robots in her class and she's decided to incorporate them during math class because math and technology are both part of STEM, which is a big emphasis in her school.

Ms. Baker planned today's lesson to be fairly quick because many students are already familiar with most of the terms. During the rest of math time, students will get a chance to use the coding robots. She begins class by introducing today's math vocabulary words: line, line segment, ray, angle, acute angle, obtuse angle, and right angle. Ms. Baker projects each vocab word on the interactive whiteboard and students take turns reading the definitions aloud. After reading each vocabulary term, she calls on a student to come to the whiteboard and show how to draw particular types of lines and angles.

Once the class is done with vocabulary, and showing how to draw different types of lines and angles, Ms. Baker shows slides with images of various polygons and asks students questions about types of angles in each polygon (acute, obtuse, right). When they are done with the slides, Ms. Baker passes out a worksheet with exercises that require students to draw and identify lines and angles. She gives them five minutes to work and announces that their homework will be to finish the worksheet. As they put their worksheets in their folders, Ms. Baker announces that for the rest of math class they'll get a chance to try out the new robots . The students seem excited and eager to get started.

At the front of the room, Ms. Baker shows one of the robots, shows them the app they can use to control the robot, and demonstrates how they can trace shapes on the screen, and the robot will follow the path they create. To connect with today's math lesson, she shows that they can draw line segments and different types of angles as paths for the robots to follow.

Then, she puts students in groups of 4–5 and tells them that they will take turns in their groups controlling the robots. Each student will have about five minutes to explore with the robots, and each group will stay in a specific area of the classroom. Next, she gives each group an iPad and a robot, and directs them toward a corner of the room where they will explore for the rest of math class. She goes from group to group ensuring that students are engaged, on task, and taking turns appropriately.

With just a few minutes left, Ms. Baker calls the students back to their desks and directs them to place the iPads and robots on her desk along the way. She asks students to share about their experiences with the robots. Much to her liking, all of the students describe how much fun they had playing with the robots.

Ms. Baker concludes the lesson optimistic about using the new coding robots frequently for the rest of the year.

Reflection Questions

Consider Ms. Baker's use of technology in this lesson. She explicitly defined a technology goal and was enthusiastic about incorporating a new tool in her math class.

- Would you consider this a technology-rich lesson? Why or why not?

- What was the purpose of Ms. Baker's technology use in this lesson?

- How did Ms. Baker's integration of technology advance the teaching and learning of math in this lesson?

- What were she and/or the class able to do with technology that was different from or better than what could have been done without technology?

- Were there any downsides to Ms. Baker's incorporation of technology in this lesson?

Consider the math teaching practices in Ms. Baker's lesson.

- What were Ms. Baker's math goals for this lesson?

- Would you say that this lesson exemplifies what it means to teach and learn math with technology? Why or why not?

- To what extent did students have equitable access to learn and demonstrate their understanding in this lesson?

- Overall, what strengths do you see in this lesson? What opportunities do you notice?

Mr. Garza's fourth-grade class is learning to draw and identify lines and angles. As you read about Mr. Garza's lesson, consider how he teaches math with technology. Take note of the opportunities students have to learn math with technology, and how it contributes to the lesson objectives.

 CASE 6.2

Mr. Garza's Grade 4 Lesson on Drawing and Identifying Lines and Angles

OBJECTIVES

- Draw lines, line segments, rays, and angles
- Identify angles and lines in polygons
- Explore new coding robots

It's near the end of the school year and Mr. Garza's class is working on a geometry unit. Today, they will learn to draw different types of lines and angles, and to identify lines and angles in polygons. In addition, students will have a chance to work with some new coding robots Mr. Garza checked out from their school's technology coach.

A couple of months ago, Mr. Garza read an article about coding in elementary classes. He was surprised to learn that young children were writing programs that created on-screen animations and manipulated robots! Although he knew very little about coding himself, he wanted to know more, so he met with the school technology coach. The coach pointed him toward some coding robots that can be controlled with a variety of apps. Mr. Garza began experimenting with the Dash robots. First, he used the Path app, where he could draw paths on the screen and drag and drop various sounds and features along the paths. Although it was fun, and he thought students would like the Paths app, he didn't see obvious connections with what his students were learning in class. Experimenting with Path gave Mr. Garza a better sense of what the Dash robot could do, so next he began playing with the Blockly app. With Blockly, Mr. Garza was able to drag and drop puzzle pieces to write programs that would move and animate Dash. The coding blocks included specified movements and turns involving lengths and angles. He immediately recognized potential connections to the geometry unit that was coming up soon. Mr. Garza talked to the technology coach about checking out more Dash robots and iPads for his class to use and began planning a lesson in which his students would use coding robots to learn about lines and angles.

Mr. Garza knew that the Grade 3 math curriculum had introduced students to lines, line segments, and types of angles. He expected many students had forgotten what some of the terms meant, so he gave a quick pre-assessment at the end of the previous day's class. From this, he learned that most students did not know all of the vocabulary, so he planned to begin the class with a review. The pre-assessment also helped him to make strategic grouping decisions for the robot activity.

The class begins with a five-minute instructional video from learnzillion.com. The video explains and illustrates the definitions of points, lines, line segments, and rays. Mr. Garza pauses the video after some of the key questions so that students can discuss their answers with a peer. After the video, he writes four additional terms on the interactive whiteboard: angle, acute, obtuse, and right. He asks students to explain what an angle is and invites three students to draw examples of angles on the board. As he points to students' angle drawings, Mr. Garza shares the definition from their textbook: "An angle is formed by two rays that share a common point, or vertex." Next, Mr. Garza draws examples of acute, obtuse, and right angles under the terms on the whiteboard. He asks students what they notice about the three examples, and what the terms above them might mean.

Sonny explains first. "The first angle is more narrow, the second one is bigger, and the last one is a corner."

"Let's talk more about that last one. Sonny, you said the third angle is a corner. I agree, but it's also a special kind of corner. Can anyone add to what Sonny said?" Mr. Garza waits until most students have their hands up and then calls on Alyson.

"I think when it's a corner like that, it's a 90 degree angle. Because when we learned about rectangles, they had to have four 90 degree angles, which are the same kind of corners."

Mr. Garza elaborates, "Yes, so what Sonny and Alyson have said is correct. An angle that is the same as the corner of a rectangle or square is a 90 degree angle. We also call a 90 degree angle a right angle. If a right angle is 90 degrees, Eli, what can you tell us about an obtuse angle?"

Eli responds, "Well, if that is a 90 degree angle, then the fatter angle is going to be more. That must mean that an obtuse angle is more than 90 degrees?"

"Exactly!" replies Mr. Garza. "And what do you think about acute angles, Rachelle?"

"Acute angles are less than 90 degrees because they are smaller."

Mr. Garza affirms Rachelle's explanation, and writes "90°" next to the right angle, "less than 90°" next to the acute angle, and "greater than 90°" next to the obtuse angle. He then lets the class know that they'll be using what they know about lines and angles to draw pictures with coding robots for the rest of class. He takes out a Dash robot and his iPad and projects the Blockly app onto the board. He shows the class what Blockly looks like, how to get started, how the puzzle pieces fit together to create programs, and tells them that they'll be starting all of their programs with the "When Start" block (see Figure 6.1). He drags and drops blocks to create the following program, and asks the class what they think Dash will do when he presses start.

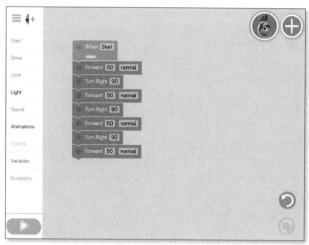

Figure 6.1 Mr. Garza's Blockly program for Dash.

Many students accurately predict that Dash will move in a square. To test their prediction, Mr. Garza presses start and the class watches as the Dash robot appears to move in a square. Next, Mr. Garza demonstrates what he will have students do during their activity. He lays out a large piece of paper on the floor, tapes a marker to Dash, and places Dash on the paper. "What do you think will happen when I press start now?" he asks. Many students exclaim, "It will draw a square on the paper!" He confirms their hypothesis by pressing start, and the class watches while the robot draws a square.

After the Dash and Blockly demonstration, Mr. Garza explains the math activity. Students will be working in groups of four to five, and each group will have a Dash robot, an iPad, a marker, a large piece of paper, some tape, and a set of numbered index cards with coding challenges. Each student receives a worksheet to record some of their thinking and results. The directions are for each group to use Blockly and Dash to draw the lines, angles, and shapes described on their index cards in order of the numbers on the cards. Before moving on to the next card, students should answer the questions on their worksheet. Mr. Garza explains that more paper is available if students need it and that he'll be walking around the room to answer questions and see how everyone is doing. He then assigns groups and hands out materials. Student groups find workspace in the classroom and get started.

Mr. Garza circulates around the class and listens in on different groups' conversations. Based on pre-assessment results, he varied the level of challenge for each group's tasks. He wanted to be sure all students could explore with the robots and learn about lines and angles without getting too frustrated to be productive. Most groups had no trouble completing card one, which asks them to draw a line of a specified length. As expected, many students are struggling with subsequent cards that involve creating angles. Although 90 degree turns work as expected, some students quickly discover that the size of Dash's turn is not the same as the acute or obtuse angle they expect to see on the paper.

Mr. Garza visits Lucy, Von, Deandre, and Tonia's group while they work on card three: "Draw a polygon that has at least one acute angle, one obtuse angle, and four or more sides (line segments)." Lucy and Von are sketching shapes on paper to figure out a shape that would meet the criteria. Meanwhile, Tonia has the iPad and is creating a program while discussing with Deandre. They appear to be using a trial-and-error strategy, repeatedly adjusting the angle measure of a turn to see what results in an acute angle. Tonia started with the code shown in Figure 6.2, which did not result in the angle they expected to see.

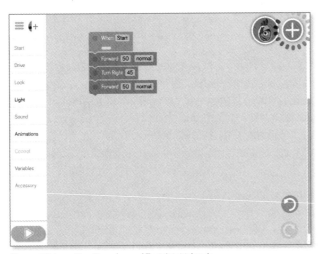

Figure 6.2 Lucy, Von, Deandre, and Tonia's initial code.

She and Deandre are discussing why the 45 degree turn and 50 steps forward ended up making an obtuse angle, even though 45 degrees should be an acute angle. Tonia quickly changes it from 45 degrees to 90 degrees, puts the robot back where it was, and says, "See, if I make it 90 degrees, then it does what it's supposed to and makes a right angle. This doesn't make any sense."

Deandre asks, "What happens if you make it bigger than 90?" Tonia tries a turn of 105 to see what happens, as shown in Figure 6.3.

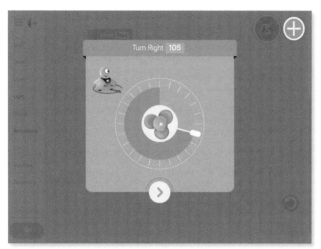

Figure 6.3 Changing Dash to rotate 105 degrees.

They still seem unsure, and keep trying with bigger numbers. Each time they notice that the bigger Dash's turn, the smaller the resulting angle. Tonia thinks aloud, "When the turn is bigger than 90, Dash turns so far that it's kind of heading back where it originally was, and the angle gets smaller." Deandre suggests that they go with a turn of 120 degrees and see what happens. After listening to this exchange and observing Lucy and Von's drawings, Mr. Garza suggests that Tonia and Deandre discuss their challenge with the rest of their group members.

Lucy and Von have sketched out a parallelogram and explain that it meets the challenge requirements: it has at least four sides, two of the angles inside the shape are obtuse, and the other two angles are acute. They explain their picture to Tonia and Deandre who agree that their polygon will meet the task criteria. Deandre points at one of the acute angles and asks, "But if this is an acute angle, why does the robot not point in the direction we want when we put in a turn less than 90?" Von begins to act out the movements. First, he walks forward. Then he turns right, less than 90 degrees. Lucy explains, "Von's turn was an acute angle. But if you're facing forward, then after you turn, you end up facing out and down a little bit so when you go forward, it makes an obtuse angle inside the shape you're drawing."

Tonia chimes in, "That's what I was saying before. When the turn is bigger than 90 degrees, Dash ends up pointing back in and you get an acute angle."

Lucy uses arrows and adds to her sketch to help the group continue making sense of their challenge. "So let's say this first line is 30 long, and then Dash turns 45 degrees right and goes forward another 30. Then the robot is going to end up here, and the drawing is going to look like this [pointing toward her picture]. But if Dash turns 150 degrees and goes forward another 30, it's going to look more like the original picture."

Tonia creates a program to reflect what Lucy just explained. The whole group cheers as Dash creates the acute angle they had hoped to draw. Now, they must figure out what kind of turn will create an obtuse angle. Tonia drags and attaches "Forward" and "Turn Right" blocks to their existing program. Deandre says, "Because we turned 150 degrees to get the acute angle, I think we will turn a lot less to get the obtuse angle."

Anticipating where their conversation might be heading, Mr. Garza tells the group, "It might help you to know that a straight line is a 180 degree angle. You might think about putting two right angles together. So if you add a 90 degree angle and a 90 degree angle, you get a 180 degree angle, or a straight line. See if that helps you figure out where to go next."

Lucy goes back to her sketch and begins to write in numbers. She explains to the group, "Dash turned 150 degrees, so from here to here is 150. And if the whole amount is 180 degrees, that must mean that the angle inside is 30 degrees. Now, with Dash facing this direction, if it makes a 30 degree turn, I think the inside will be 150 degrees. Can we try that and see if it works?" Tonia tries Lucy's suggestion and the group watches as Dash draws the third side of their parallelogram.

Von has an idea. "Because this angle is the same as the first one, we should be able to do another 150 degree turn and go forward 30 steps." Tonia adds two more blocks, presses start, and Dash turns and creates the fourth side of the group's parallelogram. With all of the steps figured out, the group places Dash on a blank part of the paper and tests to see that their program will draw a parallelogram in one series of movements. After successfully doing so, the students celebrate and begin recording their work (shown in Figure 6.4) on their worksheets.

As class time comes to an end, Mr. Garza asks students to wrap up whatever challenge they are working on and begin picking up their materials. Most of the students are reluctant to stop what they are doing, but Mr. Garza can see that they are engaged in interesting conversations about angles and lines. He tells students that they will get a chance to work with the robots again in this unit and asks everyone to turn in their worksheets, and to write all group member names on the papers where Dash drew shapes. Tomorrow, he plans to start class with a discussion of some of the Dash shape drawings and extend the activity to introduce parallel and perpendicular lines. He'll also invite some students to show their programs to the rest of the class so they can discuss how different blocks could be used to draw the same types of shapes. In particular, he wants to highlight one group's discovery of the "Repeat" block and how they used it to draw a rectangle.

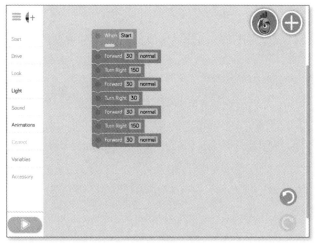

Figure 6.4 Blockly code for Dash to draw a parallelogram.

Overall, Mr. Garza feels that this lesson was a success. The students clearly enjoyed working with the robots, and their group conversations were rich with math language and problem solving. Some students would need additional support, as he could see they were still struggling to make sense of acute and obtuse angles within the coding challenges. Nevertheless, he was able to introduce straight angles to most of the groups, and they were able to use that information to make sense of the programs they were writing and the shapes that resulted. In addition to making strong progress toward today's objectives, many students also developed some understanding of supplementary angles—a term and idea that is not introduced until seventh grade! Mr. Garza looks forward to tomorrow's class discussion and to sharing the lesson success with the technology coach.

Reflection Questions

Consider Mr. Garza's use of technology in this lesson. As you reflect and discuss, consider what happened in Mr. Garza's lesson, and how it compares with Ms. Baker's class.

- Would you consider this a technology-rich lesson? Why or why not?

- What was the purpose of Mr. Garza's technology use in this lesson?

- How did Mr. Garza's integration of technology advance the teaching and learning of math in this lesson?

- What were he and/or the students able to do with technology that was different from or better than what could have been done without technology?

- Were there any downsides to Mr. Garza's incorporation of technology in this lesson?

Next, let's consider the math teaching practices in Mr. Garza's lesson and how they compare with the practices in the first case.

- What were Mr. Garza's math goals for this lesson?

- Would you say that this lesson exemplifies what it means to teach and learn math with technology? Why or why not?

- To what extent did students have equitable access to learn and demonstrate their understanding in this lesson?

- Overall, what strengths do you see in this lesson? What opportunities do you notice?

● ● ● ●

What Does the Research Say?

The following research supports the use of technology as an educational tool:

- Across the multiple conceptions of digital age skills, there has been a common thread of digital literacy and facility with digital age tools (Dede, 2010). A framework from the North Central Regional Educational Laboratory & Metiri Group (2003) identified digital age literacy as one of four essential digital age skills. The Organization for Economic Co-operation and Development more broadly referred to competency with using tools interactively (2005). The Partnership for 21st Century Skills (2006) specified the need for students to develop ICT literacy. One of the four components of their 2019 Framework for 21st Century Learning is Information, Media, and Technology Skills, which require particular kinds of literacies in the digital age (Battelle for Kids). The most recent ISTE Standards provide a framework for stakeholders in education to support digital age learning. The growing emphasis on preparing students to use and learn with digital technologies highlights their importance to K–12 education.

- There is a growing body of research that shows the benefits and potential for innovative tools in K–12 classrooms. Because of the variety of tools and scattershot way in which they are often implemented in schools, we look to small- and larger-scale studies involving technologies that are less typical in

K–12 classrooms. In studies where educators have experimented with tools such as robotics, drones, virtual and augmented reality, and GPS devices, results have suggested increases in student interest in STEM, willingness to engage in classroom activities, and positive perceptions toward the content they are learning. Although further research is needed regarding teaching and learning with new digital tools, existing studies paint an optimistic picture for their potential impact on teaching and learning.

- Along with the growing emphasis on digital tools, a focus on computational thinking in both research and practice has emerged. ISTE includes Computational Thinker as a category within their Standards for Students (2016), and offers a separate document entitled, Computational Thinking Competencies for Educators. The National Research Council has convened workshops to consider the role of computational thinking in K–12 education (2010, 2011), and how it should be incorporated in school curriculum. Since the advent of programming languages decades ago, researchers have advocated for computational thinking in K–12 education, and studied cognition relating to computing in schools (e.g., Clements & Gullo, 1984; Klahr & Carver, 1988; Liao & Bright, 1991; Papert, 1980). New calls for computational thinking and computer science education have ushered in a new era of research and programs aimed at developing students' computational thinking within the K–12 school curriculum (e.g., Aho, 2012; Grover & Pea, 2013; Lye & Koh, 2014; Weintrop et al., 2016; Wing, 2006).

The following research addresses teaching and learning math with technology:

- Since its introduction in U.S. classrooms during the 1960s "new math" era, computer programming has frequently been incorporated into or associated with the school math curriculum. In the late 1960s, Seymour Papert and colleagues developed the Logo educational programming language. This approach to programming incorporated a turtle cursor and gained traction in elementary math classrooms during the 1980s. The treatment of variables, functions, algorithmic thinking, representations, feedback, and abstraction within computer programming align with important aspects of algebraic thinking. Studies involving student use of computer programing for learning math have shown it to be a productive approach to developing mathematical understanding (e.g., Clements & Gullo, 1984; Clements & Sarama, 1993, 1997; Harel & Papert, 1990; Klahr & Carver, 1988; Noss, 1986; Sutherland, 1989). The more recent resurgence of computer science in the school curriculum creates new opportunities to implement and study programming as a tool for mathematical learning (Kalelioğlu, 2015).

- Programming is not the only way in which students can learn math through technology. A wide variety of digital tools have been implemented and studied for their potential to support and expand student learning of math. As new math tools have emerged, so too have the possibilities for enhancing teaching and learning. When combined with effective peda-gogy, teacher professional development, school curriculum, and tools such as computer algebra systems (e.g., Heid, 1988; Heid, Blume, Hollebrands, & Piez, 2002), calculators (e.g., Doerr & Zangor, 2000; Penglase & Arnold, 1996), data analysis tools and software (e.g., Lee & Hollebrands, 2011), dynamic geometry environments (e.g., Laborde, 2000; Zbiek & Hollebrands, 2008), and other software (e.g., Lantz-Anderson, Linderoth, & Säljö, 2009; Roschelle et al., 2010) have positively impacted how and what math is learned in schools.

Reflecting on Technology in Math Teaching

Reading the cases of Ms. Baker's and Mr. Garza's fourth-grade classrooms, you prob-ably noticed big differences in how the math was taught and how technology was used to support their math teaching. In Ms. Baker's class, she taught a shorter lesson so students would have a chance to play with the coding robots. While she pointed out a potential connection between the math lesson and the robot activity, students could play with the robots without attending to drawing or identifying lines and angles. Mr. Garza was also enthusiastic about incorporating coding robots in his classroom, but he designed an activity where students deepened their understanding of lines and angles by using the robots to draw shapes. The teachers in both cases emphasized similar math content and used the same kinds of technologies (interac-tive whiteboards, iPads, and coding robots). Both were technology-rich lessons, but Mr. Garza integrated and used the robots in a way that helped students learn about math and technology. In both situations, students worked in groups and seemed to have equitable opportunities to interact with the technology. In Mr. Garza's class, the math tasks students completed with technology were differentiated according to students' performance on a pre-assessment, thereby tailoring the experiences more to students' individualized needs. At the end of each lesson, Ms. Baker and Mr. Garza seemed pleased with students' engagement and eager to find more class time for students to work with these new digital tools.

TABLE 6.1 Use of Technology in the Cases of Ms. Baker and Mr. Garza

	The Case of Ms. Baker	The Case of Mr. Garza
What technology is used?	Interactive whiteboard, iPads, coding robots	Interactive whiteboards, iPads, coding robots
What math is emphasized?	Drawing and identifying lines, line segments, and types of angles.	Drawing and identifying lines, line segments, and types of angles.
How is the lesson launched?	Ms. Baker shows vocabulary words and their definitions, and invites students to the board to draw lines and angles.	Mr. Garza shows a video that reviews and explains vocabulary terms many students have forgotten. He then explains types of angles, inviting students to draw and discuss angles on the board.
Who is doing the math in this lesson?	Students apply what they see and hear at the beginning of the lesson to complete a worksheet about drawing and identifying lines and angles.	Students work in groups to complete a series of coding robot challenges that involve drawing lines, angles, and shapes that meet specific math criteria. They record some of their thinking individually, on worksheets.
When and how is technology used in the lesson?	An interactive whiteboard is used to display vocabulary terms and demonstrate how to draw lines and angles. iPads are used to explore making paths and movements with coding robots.	An interactive whiteboard is used to display a video about vocabulary terms, and demonstrate how to draw lines and angles. iPads are used to create block programs for coding robots to draw lines and angles.

One way of thinking about the contrast between Ms. Baker's and Mr. Garza's technology use in these lessons is to ask: *"Are students learning how to use technology during math, or are they learning math through using technology?"* Ms. Baker saw some connections between her math lesson and the coding robots she was eager to use in her classroom, but the learning activity did not emphasize those potential connections. On the other hand, Mr. Garza designed an activity that enabled students to learn about math and coding with robots in tandem.

Equitable access to technology and math is an important consideration in any lesson. In both classrooms, multiple students participated in the beginning of the lesson, and all students had access to work with the coding robots in collaborative small groups. Mr. Garza also planned to meet students' needs by administering a pre-assessment, and designing and selecting tasks that would be appropriately challenging for all students. The robot-programming tasks students collaborated on to solve, combined with norms for classroom discussion in his classroom, sparked rich math conversations and learning opportunities for all students.

Recommendations for Practice

Ms. Baker's and Mr. Garza's lessons provide an example of what it could look like if: *Instead of using technology for its own sake, what if we used technology in the service of learning rich, interesting math?* But what can you do to transform your classroom to teach and learn with technology? Here are three suggestions for you to consider.

1. Play with new technologies that interest you so you can identify connections with your math curriculum. Reach out to colleagues and coaches to learn more about technology!

Both Ms. Baker and Mr. Garza were inspired to use coding robots in their classrooms. Attending conferences and workshops in your community or from national organizations such as ISTE or NCTM can introduce you to new technologies you may never have considered for your classroom. If you do attend a conference, check out exhibitors' booths for new ideas and try to attend at least one session about a technology you've never tried before. You can also read about new educational technologies in books and teacher journals such as *The Elementary STEM Journal, Empowered Learner,* and *Mathematics Teacher: Learning and Teaching in PK–12.* Of course, there is a wealth of resources available online as well, to learn about cutting-edge technologies that pique your interest.

Maybe you heard a plug about a new digital tool or discovered something you would like to know more about for your classroom. Colleagues are another great resource. If you have a technology coach or coordinator like Mr. Garza did, you could reach out to learn more. Even if you don't know of anyone you could reach out to, online networks of educators can provide a supportive community through blogs and social media platforms. However you choose to connect, staying abreast of educational technology innovations can expand your horizons for what technologies are available to incorporate into your teaching. Explore and play with new technologies when you get the chance so you can identify opportunities to support your teaching and students' learning. This does not necessarily mean you have to be an expert before you try out new technologies with your students. You can often design instruction that lets you learn about technology with and from your students!

2. Design technology-rich instructional activities that give students a chance to develop technological literacy at the same time they are exploring interesting math.

Once you have identified an interesting tool and had a chance to familiarize yourself with it, the next step is to connect the tool with your teaching and learning goals. Unless you have instructional time available for learning about technology, you will likely need to figure out how you can design instructional activities that enable students to learn with technology. Some educational technologies have their own curriculum materials available. Even if this is the case and you determine that the materials align with your teaching and learning needs, you must still determine how to incorporate outside resources into your math curriculum. Also ask yourself what students will need in order to learn how to use the technology itself. Ideally, digital tools will be intuitive and user-friendly enough to require minimum training for student use. If not, you'll have to make some judgment calls about how much class time is worth investing in a tool. This is often informed by how frequently and extensively you plan to use the tool.

As you design technology-rich instructional activities, some questions you might consider include:

- How familiar are students with the technologies? How much will you need to teach about the technology before students can learn with the technology?

- Is the technology helping students learn more about a mathematical idea? The mere presence of numbers or potential to connect with a math topic does not a math lesson make.

- Does the activity help students make math connections? Do not assume that students will pick up on nuanced math connections or transfer their technology experiences to their math learning. Build those opportunities into the activity and lesson.

3. When possible, give students a chance to learn with cutting edge technologies through purposeful play.

If students are excited to work with a new and novel technology, there is a good chance they will want to dive in and explore. Lengthy tutorials or step-by-step technology-use experiences can lose students' interest quickly, and before you know it, a number of them have gotten sidetracked or lost. For this reason, you may want to minimize structured tutorials and, instead, spend time establishing some baseline competencies and ground rules. Then, design instruction so that students can explore and learn through purposeful play. These experiences are often collaborative (which fits well in situations where technology device access is limited). Providing self-paced learning activities or open-ended problems that students can solve in a variety of ways gives students a chance to learn about math and technology in ways that are more responsive to individual student needs.

Connecting Cases with Standards

In this chapter, the cases of Ms. Baker and Mr. Garza demonstrate ways in which technology could be used to teach fourth-grade geometry. Following you will find Common Core State Standards for Mathematics and ISTE Standards for Students and for Educators that align, to some extent, with one or both of the cases in this chapter. It may be useful for you to discuss and consider how the case aligns with math standards in your state or district, as well as ISTE Standards for Administrators and for Coaches.

Math Content Standards

> **CCSS.MATH.CONTENT.4.G.A.1.** Draw points, lines, line segments, rays, angles (right, acute, obtuse), and perpendicular and parallel lines. Identify these in two-dimensional figures.

> **CCSS.MATH.CONTENT.4.MD.C.5.** Recognize angles as geometric shapes that are formed whenever two rays share a common endpoint, and understand concepts of angle measurement.

> **CCSS.MATH.CONTENT.4.MD.C.7.** Recognize angle measure as additive. When an angle is decomposed into non-overlapping parts, the angle measure of the whole is the sum of the angle measures of the parts. Solve addition and subtraction problems to find unknown angles on a diagram in real world and math problems, (e.g., by using an equation with a symbol for the unknown angle measure).

Mathematical Practice Standards

- Make sense of problems and persevere in solving them
- Reason abstractly and quantitatively
- Use appropriate tools strategically
- Attend to precision

ISTE Standards for Educators

1c.   Pursue professional interests by creating and actively participating in local and global learning networks.

2c.   Model for colleagues the identification, exploration, evaluation, curation and adoption of new digital resources and tools for learning.

4a.   Dedicate planning time to collaborate with colleagues to create authentic learning experiences that leverage technology.

5b.   Design authentic learning activities that align with content area standards and use digital tools and resources to maximize active, deep learning.

6a.   Foster a culture where students take ownership of their learning goals and outcomes in both independent and group settings.

6c.   Create learning opportunities that challenge students to use a design process and computational thinking to innovate and solve problems.

7a.   Provide alternative ways for students to demonstrate competency and reflect on their learning using technology.

ISTE Standards for Students

1d.   Students understand the fundamental concepts of technology operations, demonstrate the ability to choose, use and troubleshoot current technologies and are able to transfer their knowledge to explore emerging technologies.

4b.   Students select and use digital tools to plan and manage a design process that considers design constraints and calculated risks.

4d.   Students exhibit a tolerance for ambiguity, perseverance and the capacity to work with open-ended problems.

5a.   Students formulate problem definitions suited for technology-assisted methods such as data analysis, abstract models and algorithmic thinking in exploring and finding solutions.

5c.   Students break problems into component parts, extract key information, and develop descriptive models to understand complex systems or facilitate problem-solving.

A TOOL FOR INTEGRATING TECHNOLOGY INTO YOUR MATH CLASSROOM

● Technology-rich math lessons require teachers to consider
● at least two dimensions: technology integration and math
● teaching practices.

THE GOAL THROUGHOUT THIS BOOK has been to bridge research and practice about educational technology and math teaching and learning. Chapters two through six include a total of ten different classroom cases including kindergarten and grades two through five. In each chapter, the paired cases highlighted technology use for common math goals, but the ways in which technology combined with effective teaching practices differed. Whereas the first case in each chapter highlighted common, well-intentioned uses of technology in elementary math classrooms, the second case provided a vision for what more transformative technology use might look like when combined with best practices for teaching math.

Table 7.1 summarizes the grade levels, math content, and technology availability in the classroom cases. As you have read, the previous chapters include a variety of math topics and technology availability scenarios. Classroom cases illustrate that effective math teaching with technology does not necessarily require having more technology, but rather leveraging available technologies in effective ways. Students do not need 1:1 laptops or tablets in order for elementary teachers to integrate technology into math lessons. Conversely, having technology in the classroom does not necessarily mean that its use positively impacts the teaching and learning of math.

TABLE 7.1 Grade Level, Math Content, and Technology Availability in Cases

Chapter and Grade Level	Teacher	Math Content	Technology Availability
Chapter Two: Grade Two	Ms. Stenberg	Number and Operations in Base Ten: Subtraction	Shared classroom computers
	Ms. Vaughan		Shared student laptops
Chapter Three: Grade Three	Ms. Anthony	Number and Operations Fractions: Equivalent fractions	1:1 student laptops
	Ms. Gonzales		Paired student laptops
Chapter Four: Kindergarten	Mr. Evers	Geometry: Identifying shapes	Teacher iPad; Shared classroom computers
	Ms. Jennings		Teacher computer; Shared student iPads
Chapter Five: Grade Five	Ms. Dylan	Measurement and Data: Line plots	Bring-your-own-device (BYOD) or shared classroom tablets
	Mr. Harriet		BYOD or shared classroom tablets
Chapter Six: Grade Four	Ms. Baker	Geometry: Lines and angles	Shared student iPads
	Mr. Garza		Shared student iPads

Technology-rich math lessons require teachers to consider at least two dimensions: technology integration and math teaching practices. An impactful tool for supporting teachers with evaluating and selecting technology emerged from research with a colleague (Thomas & Edson, 2017). The Digital Instructional Material Framework combines technology integration and effective math teaching practices in a matrix. Within this framework, we consider three levels of technology integration: replacement, amplification, and transformation (Hughes, Thomas, & Scharber, 2006). Replacement refers to technology integration that replaces non-tech resources, but with little value added. Amplification integration results in a noticeable enhancement. Transformation enables experiences that would not be possible without technology. The second dimension provides an object for what is to be replaced, amplified, or transformed through technology integration. We highlight the eight effective math teaching practices as defined by NCTM (2014).

The resulting framework is a matrix, which teachers or stakeholders can use to evaluate or plan for technology-rich math instruction. If you think back to some of the cases highlighted in this book, you might find it more difficult to place the first cases in each chapter on this framework, as compared with the second cases. For example, in Chapter Six, Ms. Baker used coding robots in her lesson about lines and angles, but can you identify any teaching practices that were replaced, amplified, or transformed through her use of the robots? Mr. Garza also used coding robots for similar purposes, but you might say that the robots amplified or transformed how he implemented tasks that promoted reasoning and problem solving or amplified using and connecting mathematical representations.

TABLE 7.2 Digital Instructional Material Framework

	Replacement	Amplification	Transformation
Establish math goals to focus learning			
Implement tasks that promote reasoning and problem solving			
Use and connect math representations			
Facilitate meaningful mathematical discourse			
Pose purposeful questions			
Build procedural fluency from conceptual understanding			
Support productive struggle in learning math			
Elicit and use evidence of student thinking			

The Digital Instructional Material Framework is a tool you can use in your classroom or school to help identify or evaluate the impact of technology integration on your math teaching practices. If you are more familiar with the

Substitution-Augmentation-Modification-Redefinition (SAMR) model, you might think about four columns of technology integration, rather than the three listed in the matrix. Likewise, if you integrate technology into a science, social studies, or reading class, look to standards and professional organizations to identify teaching practices outside of math.

In addition to the dimensions shown in the Digital Instructional Material Framework, teachers and stakeholders must consider a number of overarching concerns including equity and access, and incorporating technology with existing curriculum. Each chapter specifically attends to equity and access, highlighting ways that technology and teaching practices can meet individual students' needs. Technology can be a tool that provides students more access to interesting math, or it can function as a reward or a gatekeeper that denies access to some students. If technology is truly used as a learning tool, then it must be integrated in ways that alleviate, not exacerbate, inequities among students.

Integrating technology into existing math curriculum is another practical challenge, especially at the elementary level where math textbook implementation expectations tend to be high. Some curricula include technology components, but it is up to teacher and administrators to determine the value added by those resources. This book identifies a number of potentially valuable resources, but the digital age has placed new burdens on teachers to act as curators of the vast wealth of digital resources available online. Determining how and which resources fit with adopted curriculum materials requires professional knowledge and discretion. It is the author's sincere hope that this book contributes to your purposeful selection and implementation of digital resources for effectively teaching math in the future.

REFERENCES

Aho, A. V. (2012). Computation and computational thinking. *Computer Journal, 55,* 832-835.

Akçayır, M., & Akçayır, G. (2017). Advantages and challenges associated with augmented reality for education: A systematic review of the literature. *Educational Research Review, 20,* 1-11.

An, S., & Wu, Z. (2012). Enhancing mathematics teachers' knowledge of students' thinking from assessing and analyzing misconceptions in homework. *International Journal of Science and Mathematics Education, 10,* 717-753.

Atkinson, C. (1942). Radio in the classroom: Best current practices and theories. *The Clearing House, 16*(5), 291-293.

Baroody, A. J., Purpura, D. J., Eiland, M. D., Reid, E. E., & Paliwal, V. (2016). Does fostering reasoning strategies for relatively difficult basic combinations promote transfer by K–3 students? *Journal of Educational Psychology, 108*(4), 576-591.

Batelle for Kids. (2019). *Framework for 21st Century Learning.* Partnership for 21st Century Learning. Retrieved from http://www.battelleforkids.org/networks/p21/frameworks-resources

Beatty, R., & Geiger, V. (2009). Technology, communication, and collaboration: Re-thinking communities of inquiry, learning, and practice. In C. Hoyles, J.B. Lagrange (Eds.) *Mathematics Education and Technology-Rethinking the Terrain* (pp. 251-284). Boston, MA: Springer.

Berry, R. Q. III, & Ellis, M. W. (2013). Multidimensional teaching. *Mathematics Teaching in the Middle School, 19*(3), 172-178.

Black, P., & Wiliam, D. (1998a). Inside the black box: Raising standards through classroom assessment. *Phi Delta Kappan, 80*(1), 139-48.

Black, P., & Wiliam, D. (1998b). Assessment and classroom learning. *Assessment in Education, 5*(1), 7-74.

Boaler, J. (2015). Fluency without fear: Research evidence on the best ways to learn math facts. Retrieved from https://www.youcubed.org/evidence/fluency-without-fear/

Borba, M. C., Askar, P., Engelbrecht, J., Gadanidis, G., Llinares, S., & Aguilar, M. S. (2016). Blended learning, e-learning and mobile learning in mathematics education. *ZDM, 48*(5), 589-610.

Bray, W. S. (2013). How to leverage the potential of mathematical errors. *Teaching Children Mathematics, 19*(7), 424-431.

Burger, W. B., & Shaughnessy, J. M. (1986). Characterizing the van Hiele levels of development in geometry. *Journal for Research in Mathematics Education, 17*(1), 31-48.

Carnahan, C., Crowley, K., Hummel, L., & Sheehy, L. (2016, March). New perspectives on education: Drones in the classroom. In *Society for Information Technology & Teacher Education International Conference* (pp. 1920-1924). Association for the Advancement of Computing in Education (AACE).

Chapin, S. H., O'Connor, C., & Anderson, N. C. (2013). *Talk moves: A teacher's guide for using classroom discussions in math, Grades K–6*. Sausalito, CA: Math Solutions.

Clements, D. H. & Gullo, D. F. (1984). Effects of computer programming on young children's cognitions. Journal of Educational Psychology, 76, 1051-1058.

Clements, D. H. & Sarama, J. (1993). Research on Logo: Effects and efficacy. *Journal of Computing in Childhood Education, 3-4*, 263-290.

Clements, D. H. & Sarama, J. (1997). Computers support algebraic thinking. *Teaching Children Mathematics, 3*, 320-325.

Clements, D. H., & Sarama, J. (2009). *Learning and teaching early math: The learning trajectories approach*. New York, NY: Routledge.

Choppin, J. (2011). The impact of professional noticing on teachers' adaptations of challenging tasks. *Mathematical Thinking and Learning, 13*(3), 175-197.

Cobb, P. (1994). Where is the mind? Constructivist and sociocultural perspectives on mathematical development. *Educational Researcher, 23*(7), 13-20.

Cross, D. I., Hudson, R. A., Adefope, O., Lee, M. Y., Rapacki, L., & Perez, A. (2012). Success made probable: African-American girls' exploration in statistics through project-based learning. *Journal of Urban Mathematics Education, 5*(2), 55-86.

Darling-Hammond, L. (2010). Teacher education and the American future. *Journal of Teacher Education, 61*(1-2), 35-47.

Davis, J., & Martin, D. B. (2018). 2008-Racism, assessment, and instructional practices: Implications for mathematics teachers of African American students. *Journal of Urban Mathematics Education, 11*(1–2).

Dede, C. (2010). Comparing frameworks for 21st century skills. *21st century skills: Rethinking how students learn, 20,* 51-76.

Dewey, J. (1902). *The child and the curriculum.* Chicago, IL: The University of Chicago Press.

Dishon, G. (2017). New data, old tensions: Big data, personalized learning, and the challenges of progressive education. *Theory and Research in Education, 15*(3), 272-289.

Doerr, H. M., & Zangor, R. (2000). Creating meaning for and with the graphing calculator. *Educational Studies in Mathematics, 41*(2), 143-163.

Eguchi, A. (2014, July). Robotics as a learning tool for educational transformation. In *Proceeding of 4th international workshop teaching robotics, teaching with robotics & 5th international conference robotics in education, Padova (Italy)* (pp. 27-34).

Erlwanger, S. H. (1973). Benny's conception of rules and answers in IPI mathematics. *Journal of Children's Mathematical Behavior, 1,* 7-26.

Faber, J. M., Luyten, H., & Visscher, A. J. (2017). The effects of a digital formative assessment tool on mathematics achievement and student motivation: Results of a randomized experiment. *Computers & Education, 106,* 83-96.

Fehr, H. F., & Fey, J. (1969). The secondary school mathematics curriculum improvement study. *The American Mathematical Monthly, 76*(10), 1132-1137.

Ferrini-Mundy, J., & Martin, W. G. (2000). *Principles and standards for school mathematics.* Reston, VA: National Council of Teachers of Mathematics (NCTM).

Franke, M., Webb, N., Chan, A., Battey, D., Ing, M., Freund, D., & De, T. (2009). Eliciting student thinking in elementary mathematics classrooms: Practices that support understanding. *Journal of Teacher Education, 60,* 380-392.

Franklin, C., Kader, G., Mewborn, D., Moreno, J., Peck, R., Perry, M., & Schaeffer, R. (2005). *Guidelines for assessment and instruction in statistics education (GAISE) report: A Pre-K–12 curriculum framework.* Alexandria, VA: American Statistical Association.

Fuson, K. C., & Murata, A. (2007). Integrating NRC principles and the NCTM Process Standards to form a class learning path model that individualizes within whole-class activities. *National Council of Supervisors of Mathematics Journal of Mathematics Education Leadership,* 10(1), 72-91.

Galbraith, P. & Haines, C. (1998). Disentangling the nexus: Attitudes to mathematics and technology in a computer learning environment. *Educational Studies in Mathematics,* 35(3), 275-290.

Geist, E. (2010). The anti-anxiety curriculum: Combating math anxiety in the classroom. *Journal of Instructional Psychology,* 37(1), 24-31.

Gobert, J. D., Sao Pedro, M. A., Baker, R. S., Toto, E., & Montalvo, O. (2012). Leveraging educational data mining for real-time performance assessment of scientific inquiry skills within microworlds. *Journal of Educational Data Mining,* 4(1), 111-143.

Gohl, E. M., Gohl, D., & Wolf, M. A. (2009). Assessments and technology: A powerful combination for improving teaching and learning. In L. M. Pinkus (Ed.) *Meaningful measurement: The role of assessments in improving high school education in the twenty-first century* (pp. 183-197). Washington, DC: Alliance for Excellent Education.

Goos, M., Galbraith, P., Renshaw, P., & Geiger, V. (2000). Reshaping teacher and student roles in technology-enriched classrooms. *Mathematics Education Research Journal,* 12(3), 303-320.

Granito, M. & Chernobilsky, E. (2012). The effect of technology on a student's motivation and knowledge retention. *Northeastern Educational Research Association Proceedings* 2012.

Grover, S., & Pea, R. (2013). Computational thinking in K–12: A review of the state of the field. *Educational Researcher,* 42(1), 38-43.

Gutstein, E., & Peterson, B. (2013). Introduction. In E. Gutstein & B. Peterson (Eds.), *Rethinking mathematics: Teaching social justice by the numbers,* 2nd ed (pp. xi-xiii). Milwaukee, WI: Rethinking Schools.

Harel, I., & Papert, S. (1990). Software design as a learning environment. *Interactive Learning Environments, 1,* 1-32.

Hattie, J. A. C. (2009). *Visible learning: A synthesis of over 800 meta-analyses relating to achievement.* New York, NY: Routledge.

Heid, M. K. (1988). Re-sequencing skills and concepts in applied calculus using the computer as a tool. *Journal for Research in Mathematics Education, 19*(1), 3-25.

Heid, M. K., Blume, G., Hollebrands, K., & Piez, C. (2002). Implications from research on the use of CAS in the teaching and learning of mathematics. *Mathematics Teacher, 95*(8), 586-591.

Hoadley, C. M., Hsi, S., & Berman, B. P. (1995). The Multimedia Forum Kiosk and SpeakEasy, *Proceedings of ACM Multimedia.* New York, NY: ACM Press.

Hsi, S., & Hoadley, C. M. (1997). Productive discussions in science: Gender equity through electronic discourse. *Journal of Science Education and Technology, 6,* 23-36.

Hughes, J., Thomas, R., & Scharber, C. (2006). Assessing technology integration: The RAT—replacement, amplification, and transformation—framework. In C. Crawford, R. Carlsen, K. McFerrin, J. Price, R. Weber, & D. Willis (Eds.), *Proceedings of SITE 2006-Society for Information Technology & Teacher Education international conference* (pp. 1616-1620). Orlando, FL: Association for the Advancement of Computing in Education.

Hurme, T., & Jarvela, S. (2005). Students' activity in computer-supportive collaborative problem solving in mathematics. *International Journal of Computers for Mathematical Learning, 10,* 49-73.

Irving, K. E. (2006). The impact of educational technology on student achievement: Assessment. *Science Educator, 15*(1), 13-20.

International Society for Technology in Education. (1998). *National educational technology standards for students.* ISTE.

International Society for Technology in Education. (2000). *National educational technology standards for students: Connecting curriculum and technology.* ISTE.

International Society for Technology in Education. (2001). *Technology standards for school administrators (TSSA).* ISTE.

Jacobs, V.R., Lamb, L. L., & Philipp, R. A. (2010). Professional noticing of children's mathematical thinking. *Journal for Research in Mathematics Education, 41*(2), 169-202.

Kalelioğlu, F. (2015). A new way of teaching programming skills to K–12 students: Code. org. *Computers in Human Behavior, 52,* 200-210.

Kamii, C. & Dominick, A. (1998.) The harmful effects of algorithms in grades 1-4. In L. Morrow & M. Kenney (Eds.), *The teaching and learning of algorithms in school mathematics* (pp. 130-139). Reston, VA: NCTM.

Kebritchi, M., Hirumi, A., & Bai, H. (2010). The effects of modern mathematics computer games on mathematics achievement and class motivation. *Computers & Education, 55*(2), 427-443.

Kisker, E. E., Lipka, J., Adams, B. L., Rickard, A., Andrew-Ihrke, D., Yanez, E. E., & Millard, A. (2012). The potential of a culturally-based supplemental math curriculum to reduce the math performance gap between Alaska native and other students. *Journal for Research in Mathematics Education, 43*(1), 75-113.

Klahr, D., & Carver, S. M. (1988). Cognitive objectives in a LOGO debugging curriculum: Instruction, learning, and transfer. *Cognitive Psychology, 20,* 362-404.

Laborde, C. (2000). Dynamic geometry environments as a source of rich learning for the complex activity of proving. *Educational Studies in Mathematics, 44*(1-2), 151-161.

Lantz-Anderson, A., Linderoth, J., & Säljö, R. (2009). What's the problem? Meaning making and learning to do mathematical word problems in the context of digital tools. *Instructional Science, 37*(4), 325-343.

Larson, M. (2017). Breaking barriers: Actionable approaches to reach each and every learner in mathematics. Presented at Innov8 Conference, National Council of Teachers of Mathematics, Las Vegas, NV.

Leahy, S., Lyon, C., Thompson, M., & Wiliam, D. (2005). Classroom assessment: Minute by minute, day by day. Educational Leadership, 63(3), 18-24.

Lee, H. S., & Hollebrands, K. F. (2011). Characterizing and developing teachers' knowledge for teaching statistics with technology. In C. Batanero, G. Burrill, & C. Reading (Eds.), *Teaching statistics in school mathematics — Challenges for teaching and teacher education: A joint ICMI/IASE study* (pp. 359-369). New York, NY: Springer.

Lesh, R., Post, T., & Behr, M. (1987). Representations and translations among representations in mathematics learning and problem solving. In C. Janvier (Ed.) *Problems of representation in the teaching and learning of mathematics* (pp. 33-40). Hillsdale, NJ: Erlbaum.

Li, Q., & Ma, X. (2010). A meta-analysis of the effects of computer technology on school students' mathematical learning. *Educational Psychology Review, 22*(3), 215-243.

Liao, Y-K. C. & Bright, G. W. (1991). Effects of computer programming on cognitive outcomes: A meta-analysis. *Journal of Educational Computing Research, 7*(3), 251-268.

Lindvall, C. M. & Cox, R. C. (1970). *The IPI evaluation program. AERA Monograph Series on Curriculum Evaluation, No. 5.* Chicago, IL: Rand McNally and Company.

Lye, S. Y., & Koh, J. H. L. (2014). Review on teaching and learning of computational thinking through programming: What is next for K–12? *Computers in Human Behavior, 41,* 51-61.

Macfadyen, L. P., Dawson, S., Pardo, A., & Gaševic, D. (2014). Embracing big data in complex educational systems: The learning analytics imperative and the policy challenge. *Research & Practice in Assessment, 9,* 17-28.

Martin, W.G. (2009). The NCTM high school curriculum project: Why it matters to you. *Mathematics Teacher, 103*(3), 164-166.

Merchant, Z., Goetz, E. T., Cifuentes, L., Keeney-Kennicutt, W., & Davis, T. J. (2014). Effectiveness of virtual reality-based instruction on students' learning outcomes in K–12 and higher education: A meta-analysis. *Computers & Education, 70,* 29-40.

Middleton, J. A., & Spanias, P. A. (1999). Motivation for achievement in mathematics: Findings, generalizations, and criticisms of the research. *Journal for Research in Mathematics Education, 30*(1), 65-88.

Mistler-Jackson, M., & Songer, N. B. (2000). Student motivation and internet technology: Are students empowered to learn science? *Journal of Research in Science Teaching, 37*(5), 459-479.

Moreno-Armella, L., Hegedus, S., & Kaput, J. (2008). From static to dynamic mathematics: Historical and representational perspectives. *Educational Studies in Mathematics, 68,* 99-111.

Moschkovich, J. N. (1999). Understanding the needs of Latino students in reform-oriented mathematics classrooms. In L. Ortiz-Franco, N. G. Hernández, & Y. de la Cruz (Eds.), *Changing the faces of mathematics: Perspectives on Latinos* (pp. 5-12). Reston, VA: NCTM.

Moschkovich, J. (2007). Examining mathematical discourse practices. *For the Learning of Mathematics, 27*(1), 24-30.

Moschkovich, J. N. (2011). Supporting mathematical reasoning and sense making for English learners. In M.E. Strutchens & J.R. Quander (Eds.), *Focus in high school mathematics: Fostering reasoning and sense making for all students* (pp. 17-36). Reston, VA: NCTM.

Moyer, P. S. (2001). Are we having fun yet? How teachers use manipulatives to teach mathematics. *Educational Studies in Mathematics, 47*(2), 175-197.

National Council of Teachers of Mathematics. Commission on Standards for School Mathematics. (1989). *Curriculum and evaluation standards for school mathematics.* Reston, VA: Authors.

National Council of Teachers of Mathematics. (2006). *Curriculum focal points for prekindergarten through grade 8 mathematics: A quest for coherence.* Reston, VA: NCTM.

National Council of Teachers of Mathematics. (2014). *Principles to actions: Ensuring mathematical success for all.* Reston, VA: Authors.

National Mathematics Advisory Panel (NMAP). (2008). *Foundations for success: The final report of the National Mathematics Advisory Panel.* Washington, DC: U.S. Department of Education.

National Research Council. (2001a). *Adding It Up: Helping Children Learn Mathematics.* J. Kilpatrick, J. Swafford, and B. Findell (Eds.). Mathematics Learning Study Committee, Center for Education, Division of Behavioral and Social Studies and Education. Washington, DC: National Academies Press.

National Research Council. (2001b). *Knowing what students know: The science and design of educational assessment.* Washington, DC: National Academies Press.

National Research Council. (2010). *Committee for the workshops on computational thinking: Report of a workshop on the scope and nature of computational thinking.* Washington, DC: National Academies Press.

National Research Council. (2011). *Committee for the workshops on computational thinking: Report of a workshop on the scope and nature of computational thinking.* Washington, DC: National Academies Press.

North Central Regional Educational Laboratory & the Metiri Group. (2003). *enGauge 21st century skills: Literacy in the digital age.* Chicago, IL: North Central Regional Educational Laboratory.

Noss, R. (1986). Constructing a conceptual framework for elementary algebra through Logo programming. *Educational Studies in Mathematics, 17,* 335-357.

Nugent, G., Barker, B., Grandgenett, N., & Adamchuk, V. (2009, October). The use of digital manipulatives in K–12: robotics, GPS/GIS and programming. In *2009 39th IEEE Frontiers in Education Conference* (pp. 1-6). IEEE.

Olsher, S., Yerushalmy, M., & Chazan, D. (2016). How might the use of technology in formative assessment support changes in mathematics teaching? *For the Learning of Mathematics, 36*(3), 11-18.

Olson, L. (2003). Legal twists digital turns. *Education Week's Technology Counts, 22,* 11-16.

Organisation for Economic Co-operation and Development. (2005). *The definition and selection of key competencies: Executive summary.* Paris, France: OECD.

Papert, S. (1980). *Mindstorms: Children, computers, and powerful ideas.* New York, NY: Basic Books.

Partnership for 21st Century Skills. (2006). *A state leader's action guide to 21st century skills: A new vision for education.* Tuscon, AZ: Partnership for 21st Century Skills.

Pellegrino, J. W., & Quellmalz, E. S. (2010). Perspectives on the integration of technology and assessment. *Journal of Research on Technology in Education,* 43(2), 119-134.

Penglase, M., & Arnold, S. (1996). The graphics calculator in mathematics education: A critical review of recent research. *Mathematics Education Research Journal,* 8(1), 58-90.

Peters, H., Kruger, V., & Fitzpatrick, E. (2018). Creative digital technology ideas for the secondary school mathematics classroom. *Australian Mathematics Teacher, The,* 74(4), 3-8.

Piaget, J., & Duckworth, E. (1970). Genetic epistemology. *American Behavioral Scientist,* 13(3), 459-480.

Planas, N., & Civil, M. (2013). Language-as-resource and language-as-political: Tensions in the bilingual mathematics classroom. *Mathematics Education Research Journal,* 25(3), 361-378.

Popham, W. J. (2008). *Transformative assessment.* Alexandria, VA: Association for Supervision and Curriculum Development.

Riel, M. (1991). Learning circles: A functional analysis of educational telecomputing. *Interactive Learning Environments,* 2, 15-30.

Roschelle, J. M., Pea, R. D., Hoadley, C. M., Gordin, D. N., & Means, B. M. (2000). Changing how and what children learn in school with computer-based technologies. *Future of Children: Children and Computer Technology,* 10(2), 76-101.

Roschelle, J., Schechtman, N., Tatar, D., Hegedus, S., Hopkins, B., Empson, S., Knudson, J., & Gallagher, L. P. (2010). Integration of technology, curriculum, and professional development for advancing middle school mathematics: Three large-scale studies. *American Educational Research Journal,* 47(4), 833-78.

Scardamalia, M., & Bereiter, C. (1993). Technologies for knowledge-building discourse. *Communications of the ACM,* 36, 37-41.

Schifter, C., Natarajan, U., Ketelhut, D. J., & Kirschgessner, A. (2014). Data-driven decision-making: Facilitating teacher use of student data to inform classroom instruction. *Contemporary Issues in Technology and Teacher Education, 14*(4), 419-432.

Schifter, D. (2001). Learning to see the invisible: What skills and knowledge are needed to engage with students' mathematical ideas? In T. Wood, B. S. Nelson, & J. Warfield (Eds.), *Beyond classical pedagogy: Teaching elementary school mathematics,* (pp. 109-134). Mahwah, NJ: Erlbaum, 2001.

Schwendimann, B. A., Rodriguez-Triana, M. J., Vozniuk, A., Prieto, L. P., Boroujeni, M. S., Holzer, A., … & Dillenbourg, P. (2017). Perceiving learning at a glance: A systematic literature review of learning dashboard research. *IEEE Transactions on Learning Technologies, 10*(1), 30-41.

Sherin, M., Jacobs, V., & Philipp, R. (Eds.). (2011). *Mathematics teacher noticing: Seeing through teachers' eyes.* New York, NY: Routledge.

Sfard, A. (2001). There is more to discourse than meets the ears: Looking at thinking as communicating to learn more about mathematical learning. *Educational Studies in Mathematics, 46,* 13-57.

Smith, M. S., & Stein, M. K. (2011). *5 Practices for Orchestrating Productive Mathematics Discussions.* Reston, VA: National Council of Teachers of Mathematics.

Star, J. R., Chen, J. A., Taylor, M. W., Durkin, K., Dede, C., & Chao, T. (2014). Studying technology-based strategies for enhancing motivation in mathematics. International *Journal of STEM Education,* 1-7.

Sutherland, R. (1989). Providing a computer based framework for algebraic thinking. *Educational Studies in Mathematics, 20,* 317-344.

Suthers, D., Toth, E. E., & Weiner, A. (1997). An integrated approach to implementing collaborative inquiry in the classroom. *Proceedings of the Conference on Computer Supported Collaborative Learning.* Toronto, Ontario: CSCL.

Swan, M. (2001). Dealing with misconceptions in mathematics. In P. Gates (Ed.), *Issues in Mathematics Teaching* (pp. 147-165). New York, NY: Routledge.

Thomas, A. (2013). A study of Algebra 1 students' use of digital and print textbooks. (Doctoral dissertation, University of Missouri-Columbia. Columbia, MO.)

Thomas, A. (2017). Screencasting to support effective teaching practices. *Teaching Children Mathematics, 23*(8), 492-499.

Thomas, A., & Edson, A. J. (2017). A framework for mathematics teachers' evaluation of digital instructional materials: Integrating mathematics teaching practices with technology use in K–8 classrooms. In P. Resta & S. Smith (Eds.), *Proceedings of Society for Information Technology & Teacher Education international conference* (pp. 11-18). Austin, TX: Association for the Advancement of Computing in Education.

Torff, B., & Tirotta, R. (2010). Interactive whiteboards produce small gains in elementary students' self-reported motivation in mathematics. *Computers & Education, 54*(2), 37-383.

Tripathi, P. N. (2008). Developing mathematical understanding through multiple representations. *Mathematics Teaching in the Middle School, 13*(8), 438-445.

U.S. Department of Education, Office of Educational Technology. (2017). *Reimagining the role of technology in education: 2017 National Education Technology Plan update.* Washington, DC: Authors.

Vahey, P., Knudsen, J., Rafanan, K., & Lara-Meloy, T. (2012). Curricular activity systems supporting the use of dynamic representations to foster students' deep understanding of mathematics. In *Emerging technologies for the classroom* (pp. 15-30). New York, NY: Springer.

van Hiele, P. M. (1980). *Levels of thinking, how to meet them, how to avoid them.* Paper presented at the meeting of the National Council of Teachers of Mathematics, Seattle, WA.

Vygotsky, L. (1978). *Mind in society: The development of higher psychological processes.* Cambridge, MA: Harvard University Press.

Webb, M., Gibson, D., & Forkosh-Baruch, A. (2013). Challenges for information technology supporting educational assessment. *Journal of Computer Assisted Learning, 29*(5), 451-462.

Weintrop, D., Beheshti, E., Horn, M., Orton, K., Jona, K., Trouille, L., & Wilensky, U. (2016). Defining computational thinking for mathematics and science classrooms. *Journal of Science Education and Technology, 25*(1), 127-147.

White, T. (2006). Code talk: Student discourse and participation with networked handhelds. *International Journal of Computer-Supported Collaborative Learning, 1*(3), 359-382.

Wiliam, D. (2011). *Embedded Formative Assessment*. Bloomington, IN: Solution Tree Press.

Wing, J. (2006). Computational thinking. *Communications of the ACM, 49*(3), 33-36.

Xhakaj, F., Aleven, V., & McLaren, B. M. (2016). How teachers use data to help students learn: Contextual inquiry for the design of a dashboard. In *European Conference on Technology Enhanced Learning* (pp. 340-354). Springer, Cham.

Zbiek, R., & Hollebrands, K. (2008). A research-informed view of the process of incorporating mathematics technology into classroom practice by inservice and prospective teachers. In M. K. Heid & G. Blume (Eds.), *Research on technology in the learning and teaching of mathematics: Syntheses and perspectives*. Charlotte, NC: Information Age Publishers.

ISTE STANDARDS

ISTE Standards for Students

The ISTE Standards for Students emphasize the skills and qualities we want for students, enabling them to engage and thrive in a connected, digital world. The standards are designed for use by educators across the curriculum, with every age student, with a goal of cultivating these skills throughout a student's academic career.

1. Empowered Learner

Students leverage technology to take an active role in choosing, achieving and demonstrating competency in their learning goals, informed by the learning sciences. Students:

a. articulate and set personal learning goals, develop strategies leveraging technology to achieve them and reflect on the learning process itself to improve learning outcomes.

b. build networks and customize their learning environments in ways that support the learning process.

c. use technology to seek feedback that informs and improves their practice and to demonstrate their learning in a variety of ways.

d. understand the fundamental concepts of technology operations, demonstrate the ability to choose, use and troubleshoot current technologies and are able to transfer their knowledge to explore emerging technologies.

2. Digital Citizen

Students recognize the rights, responsibilities and opportunities of living, learning and working in an interconnected digital world, and they act and model in ways that are safe, legal and ethical. Students:

a. cultivate and manage their digital identity and reputation and are aware of the permanence of their actions in the digital world.

b. engage in positive, safe, legal and ethical behavior when using technology, including social interactions online or when using networked devices.

c. demonstrate an understanding of and respect for the rights and obligations of using and sharing intellectual property.

d. manage their personal data to maintain digital privacy and security and are aware of data-collection technology used to track their navigation online.

3. Knowledge Constructor

Students critically curate a variety of resources using digital tools to construct knowledge, produce creative artifacts and make meaningful learning experiences for themselves and others. Students:

a. plan and employ effective research strategies to locate information and other resources for their intellectual or creative pursuits.

a. evaluate the accuracy, perspective, credibility and relevance of information, media, data or other resources.

b. curate information from digital resources using a variety of tools and methods to create collections of artifacts that demonstrate meaningful connections or conclusions.

c. build knowledge by actively exploring real-world issues and problems, developing ideas and theories and pursuing answers and solutions.

4. Innovative Designer

Students use a variety of technologies within a design process to identify and solve problems by creating new, useful or imaginative solutions. Students:

a. know and use a deliberate design process for generating ideas, testing theories, creating innovative artifacts or solving authentic problems.

b. select and use digital tools to plan and manage a design process that considers design constraints and calculated risks.

c. develop, test and refine prototypes as part of a cyclical design process.

d. exhibit a tolerance for ambiguity, perseverance and the capacity to work with open-ended problems.

5. Computational Thinker

Students develop and employ strategies for understanding and solving problems in ways that leverage the power of technological methods to develop and test solutions. Students:

a. formulate problem definitions suited for technology-assisted methods such as data analysis, abstract models and algorithmic thinking in exploring and finding solutions.

b. collect data or identify relevant data sets, use digital tools to analyze them, and represent data in various ways to facilitate problem-solving and decision-making.

c. break problems into component parts, extract key information, and develop descriptive models to understand complex systems or facilitate problem-solving.

d. understand how automation works and use algorithmic thinking to develop a sequence of steps to create and test automated solutions.

6. Creative Communicator

Students communicate clearly and express themselves creatively for a variety of purposes using the platforms, tools, styles, formats and digital media appropriate to their goals. Students:

a. choose the appropriate platforms and tools for meeting the desired objectives of their creation or communication.

b. create original works or responsibly repurpose or remix digital resources into new creations.

c. communicate complex ideas clearly and effectively by creating or using a variety of digital objects such as visualizations, models or simulations.

d. publish or present content that customizes the message and medium for their intended audiences.

7. Global Collaborator

Students use digital tools to broaden their perspectives and enrich their learning by collaborating with others and working effectively in teams locally and globally. Students:

a. use digital tools to connect with learners from a variety of backgrounds and cultures, engaging with them in ways that broaden mutual understanding and learning.

b. use collaborative technologies to work with others, including peers, experts or community members, to examine issues and problems from multiple viewpoints.

c. contribute constructively to project teams, assuming various roles and responsibilities to work effectively toward a common goal.

d. explore local and global issues and use collaborative technologies to work with others to investigate solutions.

ISTE Standards for Educators

The ISTE Standards for Educators are your road map to helping students become empowered learners. These standards will deepen your practice, promote collaboration with peers, challenge you to rethink traditional approaches and prepare students to drive their own learning.

Empowered Professional

1. Learner

Educators continually improve their practice by learning from and with others and exploring proven and promising practices that leverage technology to improve student learning. Educators:

a. Set professional learning goals to explore and apply pedagogical approaches made possible by technology and reflect on their effectiveness.

b. Pursue professional interests by creating and actively participating in local and global learning networks.

c. Stay current with research that supports improved student learning outcomes, including findings from the learning sciences.

2. Leader

Educators seek out opportunities for leadership to support student empowerment and success and to improve teaching and learning. Educators:

a. Shape, advance and accelerate a shared vision for empowered learning with technology by engaging with education stakeholders.

b. Advocate for equitable access to educational technology, digital content and learning opportunities to meet the diverse needs of all students.

c. Model for colleagues the identification, exploration, evaluation, curation and adoption of new digital resources and tools for learning.

3. Citizen

Educators inspire students to positively contribute to and responsibly participate in the digital world. Educators:

a. Create experiences for learners to make positive, socially responsible contributions and exhibit empathetic behavior online that build relationships and community.

b. Establish a learning culture that promotes curiosity and critical examination of online resources and fosters digital literacy and media fluency.

c. Mentor students in safe, legal and ethical practices with digital tools and the protection of intellectual rights and property.

d. Model and promote management of personal data and digital identity and protect student data privacy.

Learning Catalyst

4. Collaborator

Educators dedicate time to collaborate with both colleagues and students to improve practice, discover and share resources and ideas, and solve problems. Educators:

a. Dedicate planning time to collaborate with colleagues to create authentic learning experiences that leverage technology.

b. Collaborate and co-learn with students to discover and use new digital resources and diagnose and troubleshoot technology issues.

c. Use collaborative tools to expand students' authentic, real-world learning experiences by engaging virtually with experts, teams and students, locally and globally.

d. Demonstrate cultural competency when communicating with students, parents and colleagues and interact with them as co-collaborators in student learning.

5. Designer

Educators design authentic, learner-driven activities and environments that recognize and accommodate learner variability. Educators:

Use technology to create, adapt and personalize learning experiences that foster independent learning and accommodate learner differences and needs.

Design authentic learning activities that align with content area standards and use digital tools and resources to maximize active, deep learning.

Explore and apply instructional design principles to create innovative digital learning environments that engage and support learning.

6. Facilitator

Educators facilitate learning with technology to support student achievement of the 2016 ISTE Standards for Students. Educators:

a. Foster a culture where students take ownership of their learning goals and outcomes in both independent and group settings.

b. Manage the use of technology and student learning strategies in digital platforms, virtual environments, hands-on makerspaces or in the field.

c. Create learning opportunities that challenge students to use a design process and computational thinking to innovate and solve problems.

d. Model and nurture creativity and creative expression to communicate ideas, knowledge or connections.

7. Analyst

Educators understand and use data to drive their instruction and support students in achieving their learning goals. Educators:

a. Provide alternative ways for students to demonstrate competency and reflect on their learning using technology.

b. Use technology to design and implement a variety of formative and summative assessments that accommodate learner needs, provide timely feedback to students and inform instruction.

c. Use assessment data to guide progress and communicate with students, parents and education stakeholders to build student self-direction.

INDEX

Your Opinion Matters
Tell Us How We're Doing!

Your feedback helps ISTE create the best possible resources for teaching and learning in the digital age. Share your thoughts with the community or tell us how we're doing!

You Can:

- Write a review at amazon.com or barnesandnoble.com.

- Mention this book on social media and follow ISTE on Twitter @iste, Facebook @ISTEconnects or Instagram @isteconnects

- Email us at books@iste.org with your questions or comments.